Freshers Lean

Your Lean Journey Starts Here

First edition

by

John Bicheno
Jonathan Barnett
Marjolijn Feringa
Gijs Wijers

June 2025

Title:	Freshers Lean
Subtitle:	Your Lean Journey Starts Here
Authors:	John Bicheno, Jonathan Barnett, Marjolijn Feringa and Gijs Wijers
Illustrations:	Krijn Spaapen
ISBN:	978 90 829 0081 1
Edition:	First edition, June 2025

Why not think about times to come?
And not about the things that you've done
If your life was bad to you
Just think what tomorrow will do

Don't stop thinking about tomorrow
Don't stop, it'll soon be here
It'll be better than before
Yesterday's gone, yesterday's gone

- Chris McVie, Fleetwood Mac -

Foreword from the authors

Lean is everywhere—whether we realise it or not. It's in the way we get ready in the morning, the way we plan our week, and the way we operate with people at home or at work. Yet, despite its widespread presence and relevance, Lean is often presented as complex, technical, and reserved for specialists.

This creates a barrier that prevents many people from exploring its principles, recognising them in everyday life, and then applying them in meaningful ways. Many of these barriers are unwittingly created by subject matter experts, many are created by our own disbelief that the idea of Lean and Agile are as intuitive and as obvious as they seem to be.

This book was written to break down these barriers and prove that indeed, Lean is simple, it is all around us, and with some guidance we can all recognise how valuable it can be to us in all aspects of life. Some of you are already Lean, you just didn't know you are!

We set out with a simple goal: to make Lean and Agile understandable, relatable, and accessible to everyone. By using everyday examples with your own curiosity and interest, we hope to show that Lean is not just a set of tools for factories or large corporations—it's a way of thinking that can improve how we think and behave, live and work, no matter the context.

We genuinely believe that Lean is simple, intuitive and practical, there is no reason for it to be intimidating. That's why this book deliberately avoids jargon and complexity, choosing instead to focus on the essence of Lean and Agile thinking through everyday real-life stories and familiar scenarios.

Our hope is that as you read, you'll start to see Lean all around you—and feel inspired to use it in ways that make a difference. Perhaps this is just the start of your own Lean journey.

Thank you

Creating Freshers Lean has been a journey shaped by the insights and experiences of our diverse Lean community. From discussions on what to avoid, to creative idea generation, from engaging focus groups, to the final rounds of proofreading—every step was touched by your input. At its core, this book carries the voices of real Freshers and how they felt it best to start your own Lean journey.

We'd like to say a big thank you to the following people:

Mahrokh Shiralipour, Puck Terlingen, Frances Diepstraten, Martin Yakimov, Lika Zanko, Elsa Decruppe, Manya Anand, Jasper Lasee, Hanshalika Neupane, Nina Ondrová, Hanshalika Neupane, Vicente Vasquez Fucaraccio, Isabela Salmoria de Figueiredo, Sofiia Chervonenko, Bastiaan Hoeflsoot, Nina Radder, Remco Bakker, Robin Hofmeester, Britte de Vries, Ilona Maasen, Lu dobbelsteen, Manjola Shala, Floortje Aarden, Bas van Rooijen, Edwin Koningen, Nashwa Usama, Japer Klos, Flavia Tofan, Philip Kluwer, Joshua Lobato, Nikki Hopman, Mohammadmahdi Zamani Sedeh, Anna Jacobsen, Artjom Solovei, Nikolay Chernev, Emi Uijtewaal, Pleun Kompier, Amanbir Singh, Artom Batalov, Tapas Arkae, Elizaveta Konkova.

For those we have missed, our apologies.

Table of Contents

Welcome!

So, you would like to learn about Lean and Agile? Perhaps you've heard the words in your work environment? Perhaps you're a student taking a course in which Lean and Agile are included in the curriculum? Or maybe you're just curious about Lean and Agile and would like to learn a little more?

The only pre-requisite in this publication is a mindset that is open to ideas - to be open to the *possibility* of new ideas and perspectives. We hope we can help.

Whatever your motivation for reading this text, we hope you'll come to understand Lean and Agile concepts based on your everyday experiences. We believe that Lean and Agile concepts are quite simple, effective, and proven. However, they are certainly not difficult to understand, and you may find most of this thinking completely natural. We believe that Lean and Agile is not a set of rules to obey, but a way of thinking, seeing, and behaving.

We have called this publication 'Freshers Lean'. These two words are important in conjunction with the word 'Agile':

1. **'Fresher'** is a word associated with a new student. A Fresher here may be a student at an institution but may also be an aspiring practitioner of any age who is new to the world of operations. A Fresher comes to a place of learning with curiosity and an open mind, a 'fresh' perspective, not hindered by prior knowledge or fixed ideas about life in an office, factory or other workplace,

2. **Lean** is about relentless improvement and removal of wasteful activities with strong participation from everyone. An outcome of Lean would be the continual reduction of the time from order to delivery, and improvement in quality. Lean is a journey, not a project. Its roots originated in the automotive industry, particularly in the Toyota Production System, but now you see Lean everywhere. The principles and concepts can be used in multiple work environments and, as we'll

discuss in this book, in your day-to-day life too. Lean isn't necessarily something we do; it is something we should aspire to become.

3. **Agile** has flexibility at its core, and an ability to adapt quickly and easily to changing customer requirements. The emphasis is on many short-term focused bursts of activity. Its roots lie in computer software development which grew out of older, unsatisfactory ways in which software was developed. Agile has adopted many concepts from Lean and as a result, the two form a powerful combination for increasing value in work and everyday life. Today the concepts are widely found, particularly in project management, and are no longer confined to software.

Do you believe that a work organisation should engage, listen, encourage, respect, share, be honest, and be environmentally responsible? If so, this book will be of relevance to you.

Framework

This book will discuss various concepts of Lean and Agile using the Bicycle framework below. This framework applies in most Lean and Agile situations – in private and public sector, and in service and manufacturing. Lean and Agile practitioners have both used frameworks that seek to show how the various tools or methodologies fit together.

But first, a word of caution from George Box (one of the world's greatest statisticians): 'All models are wrong. Some models are useful'. We think this model is useful.

The Chapters in this book are arranged according to this 'Bicycle' framework. We start with explaining the principles of Lean and Agile and then explain within the Chapters via Fishbone diagrams the major concepts that are used to group and consolidate.

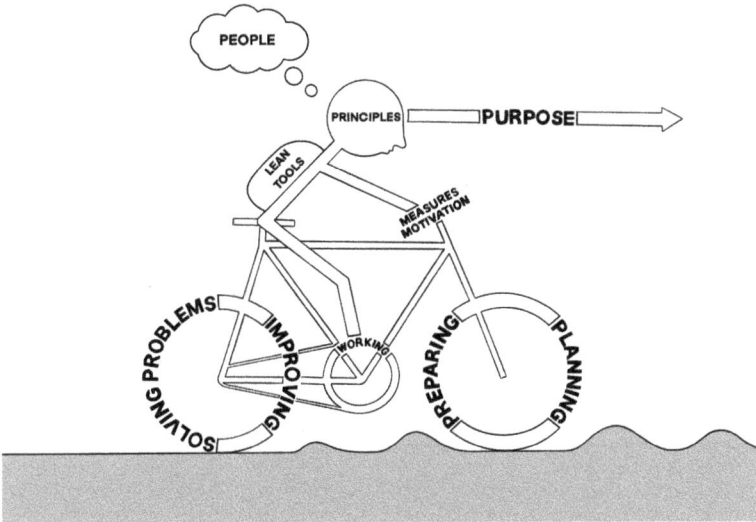

How to read the model

- There is a cyclist and a bicycle. The bicycle is no use unless it helps the cyclist to go where he or she wants to go. The cyclist is certainly helped by the bicycle, but unless the cyclist is motivated the cyclist-bicycle system is useless. In a Lean and Agile system, much attention needs to be given to 'people' aspects.
- The cyclist knows where to go. This is purpose and strategy. Scanning the horizon the cyclist steers the bike, making necessary adjustments along the way.
- The cyclist keeps track of progress (measures) and is motivated to continue.
- Working reveals problems and opportunities for improvement. In the backpack the cyclist keeps all the Lean tools, so they are available when needed.
- The wheels and the pedals are circular. Problem solving & Improving, Preparing & planning, keep going in a continuous loop.
- As the bicycle progresses down the road, bumps and obstructions are encountered. These represent instability. This will make the journey uncomfortable or unstable, so an early priority is for it to be reduced. This makes the journey easier for the cyclist who is no longer buffeted by instability. Swift, even, progression (called 'flow' In Lean) becomes more possible.
- The bicycle is on a journey. It never ends.

The framework is depicted as a bicycle. However, there are important things to note....

- These concepts are integrated because all are needed to work effectively. A 'penny-farthing' bicycle, which would represent an unbalanced system, would be almost impossible to ride. Lean is no different, the concepts need each other if the journey is going to be successful.
- Of course there is a cyclist. The concepts will not work together without people being involved to literally drive the system forward. When the cyclist stops peddling the

whole system stops. Continued involvement of people is not only required, but also essential.

To help bring the framework to life, as with many things Lean and Agile, an everyday example can be found. Let's take for example, the annual activity of going on holiday...

Going on holiday using the Bicycle Framework

Purpose of your holiday

First you need to know what you are aiming at. The 'What'. Is it also the 'Why'? 'What's' are often driven by 'Whys'? But you also have Values that guide all your subsequent actions. For example, your behaviour towards friends, customers, suppliers, the public, the environment.

Sometimes taking a break from your usual routine can be an obvious reason for a holiday, but the Purpose of a holiday can vary from person to person. The Purpose of *your* holiday can be difficult to describe to others, but it's easy to understand yourself. Perhaps it is simply to 'relax' or 'recharge your batteries'. Maybe it is to travel and experience, or in some instances, to learn. Maybe you want to explore and be challenged? It might be as simple as 'enjoy some warm weather and do absolutely nothing'. If you are planning things as a group there should be a shared purpose which can be arrived at through discussion so that everyone agrees on the purpose. This is called 'alignment' in Lean.

The Values guide and support everything that follows, much like table legs support the tabletop. The way to behave and act throughout the process should always be in support of the overall purpose.

Planning your holiday

The holiday where and when. Who will go? How to travel? Your budget. Several other considerations, such as taking leave.

For the best possible chance of achieving the purpose from the holiday, careful planning is needed. What do we need to do? Who are we going with? Do we have time available from work? What is the best way to get to our destination? How much is everything going to cost!

Once we're happy we have the list of things that need to happen, in what order do these things need to be done? Who do we need to do what and when? Maybe additional help is required for booking or arranging? Maybe your adventure needs a particular visa or perhaps specific vaccinations?

Poor planning only makes organising more challenging. Making sure throughout that both are done effectively and are in line with our Purpose and Value allows us to look forward to the event itself. If things are missed at this stage, it might be too late by the time we realise...

Preparing your holiday

What you need to pack and to wear. The timetable.

Finally, as the plans get closer to reality, we can start to prepare for the holiday itself. Have we thought about the smaller details for the trip itself? What activities are planned? What clothes are required? Have there been any changes to the weather? Let's not overlook cultural sensitivities. Are we aware of the cultural differences of our holiday destination? Is everything I'm planning to wear appropriate? Are there any risks we've overlooked such as cell phone service or perhaps emergency contacts? Perhaps it might be good to make sure we all understand some basic phrases of the language? Its way more fun planning the exciting things, but good preparation means we can't be ignorant to the risks either.

Working 'your holiday' (Make your holiday happen)

Actually going on holiday, and what to do each day.

Finally, the day arrives, all that planning and preparing has been worth it because so far, everything that was meant to happen, has happened. Plans and activities flow seamlessly from one to the next, and whilst lots of things are going on, nothing seems stressful or rushed. Everyone knows where we should be at what time, and there is plenty of free time and energy to make some last-minute adjustments if required.

Improving during your holiday

What you do to make the holiday better. Some improvements are carried out immediately; others are lessons for next time.

As the holiday progresses and is very common, especially in a group holiday or family event, mealtimes, either breakfast or the evening meal is a great opportunity to share stories and events so far. This daily catch up of sharing opinions and perspectives gives insights into the experiences of others; What went well? What would be even better if...?

Some adjustments for the very next day are possible by meeting and discussing in this way. Everyone wants to get the most out of the experience and check that we are all making sure we satisfy the purpose of the holiday. Sometimes adjustments aren't possible, and it may occur that as the days pass, the list of 'even better ifs' gets bigger and ultimately, if this sort of holiday was to be booked again "*we should definitely do things a bit differently*". This can also be discussed and indeed remembered for next time.

Motivating and Measuring during your holiday

Some in your group need motivating to 'get up and go'. Measuring means how you rate the travel, location, and activities.

Throughout Preparing and Working, there may be discussions around the level of participation from some of the people involved in the trip. Perhaps it is early in the process where agreeing dates is challenging, or perhaps agreeing location and budget. It might be just the timeliness of responding to messages and the sending of the correct details such as passport information. It can be very frustrating waiting on a response from someone when they have information you need. Some people may know exactly what they want from the trip, some may find it hard to describe.

It might be that during the trip itself planned excursions are missed due to people sleeping in too late! Even getting people to the same restaurant at the agreed time can sometimes be challenging.

The measuring of experiences is always going to be challenging. People have different perspectives of experiences and quality is always hard to measure. It can be very difficult to compare what was planned and prepared with what has actually been experienced. But the daily evening meal provides an opportunity to discuss, measure, and evaluate the main elements of the trip so far. The measures should relate to the purpose. Have we achieved what we set out to do?'

Solving Problems during your holiday

These may arise during any of the previous stages. Some problems you will be able to solve on your own, but others may require outside help.

As mentioned, improvements can be made by active participation and discussion throughout. This is often to maximise the experience. 'Fine tune' if you like. However, it may be that real problems emerge and these need to be addressed in the most effective way.

Perhaps problems emerge with conflict between people around the Purpose of the holiday, or in disagreements around budget and location. It might be a problem related to the Planning such as issues with a particular visa or required document.

Preparing presents its own challenges. Some people are more relaxed about how they prepare… Some think of every detail preparing in advance with a suitcase open at the ready and really enjoying the process. Some have more of an 'it'll be okay' attitude and prefer not to 'overthink things' and prepare at the last possible moment.

Sometimes a significant problem can arise such as an illness or a lost bank card. This is a big deal, and it isn't going to get solved without some outside assistance. Who do we need to help?

Something also to consider is that personalities play a large role in group activities such as this. People have different attitudes and perspectives, and they can sometimes change over time. Perhaps some people like to stick rigidly to the planned events, whilst some prefer to 'get lost in the moment' and change things last minute during the trip. It is critical that these sorts of issues and problems get discussed, people are listened to with humility, and problems resolved so as the whole 'Purpose' of the trip isn't lost.

People while on holiday

When you think back on the holidays you've had, you can probably remember who you went on holiday with and what kind of people you met while on holiday. And what the atmosphere was like in that holiday.

People are a defining factor. You are a human being yourself; how did you feel? Were you happy? Besides yourself it can be the people you are on holiday with, but of course also the people you just meet, for instance the staff in the hotel or restaurant. Do you feel comfortable with them? Can you do what you want to do? Are you listened to?

Fishbone

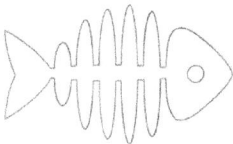

In the beginning of each Chapter the concepts will be defined, and within the Bicycle framework you'll find a fishbone structure. This is to make the different concepts clearer to you, highlighting which concepts are relevant to that particular part of the model.

Through the fishbone you can see how the concepts are related and acting in support of each element of the bicycle framework.

In the Chapter itself, they will be defined and explained, and an overview of their application.

We have also provided an everyday example of each element to help you recognise that this way of thinking and behaving is visible in everyday life.

And you can 'See for Yourself' by doing the suggested exercises.

Lean and Agile Principles

To explain about Lean and Agile a good start is to look at their principles. Both Lean and Agile have core principles. These are not in conflict with one another but are mutually reinforcing. These principles are also widely accepted in contemporary operations.

In the Bicycle framework you can find these principles literally in the head of the cyclist. While working they are always at the forefront of your mind. It is the way the cyclist will think and act. For this there is no difference between Lean and Agile.

Lean's Principles as outlined by Womack and Jones are:

1. **Value**: Determine the value from the customer's perspective and eliminate anything that does not add value.
2. **Value Stream**: Map out the entire process, from raw materials to the customer, to identify opportunities for improvement.
3. **Flow**: Ensure that the product or service flows smoothly through the process, eliminating interruptions and waste.
4. **Pull**: Produce only what is needed, when it is needed, to maintain a steady flow of value to the customer.
5. **Perfection**: Continuously improve processes and eliminate waste, aiming for perfection in the value stream.

These principles form the basis of the Lean methodology, which aims to create a more efficient and effective way of working. By following these principles, organisations can eliminate waste, reduce variability, and improve the overall value delivered to customers.

Agile Principles (Manifesto for Agile Software Development):

1. **Individuals and interactions over processes and tools**: Emphasize collaboration and communication over rigid processes and tools.
2. **Working software over comprehensive documentation**: Prioritize delivering working software over creating extensive documentation.
3. **Customer collaboration over contract negotiation**: Foster close collaboration with customers to understand their needs, rather than relying on contracts.
4. **Responding to change over following a plan**: Emphasize adaptability and responding to change, rather than rigidly following a plan.
5. **Reflecting on how to become more effective**: Continuously reflect on and improve the development process itself.

Agile Principles were first developed for software development but are now widely adapted across other industries.

The principles of Lean and Agile share some commonalities, such as a focus on continuous improvement, collaboration, and customer value. Lean emphasizes eliminating waste and improving processes, while Agile emphasizes adaptability and responding to change. By combining the principles of both methodologies, organisations can create a culture that values efficiency, flexibility, and customer satisfaction, leading to better products and services that meet customer needs.

Waste: Muda, Muri and Mura

Waste reduction is a major aim in Lean. There is a famous word for waste in Lean:

It is **Muda**. The major causes of Muda are Muri and Mura:

Muri is overload – of people, of machines, of processes. You know yourself that there is a natural limit of the amount of work that you can do well. Beyond the limit, fatigue and stress set in. This can be physical, mental, or psychological. Productivity falls, and waste results.

Mura is variation, that could be instability, interruptions, stoppages, unpredictability, or simply natural variation that everyone experiences every day. Mura is experienced by all processes and systems.

There are two types of Mura:

1. Demand variation (or external variation).
2. Process variation (or internal variation).

You need to pay attention to both. (Some men lift weights to develop their biceps. But it would be unusual to see a man with a large right bicep, but a skinny left arm!)

The point is that Muri is a major cause of Mura, and both are major causes of Muda. A diagram is shown below.

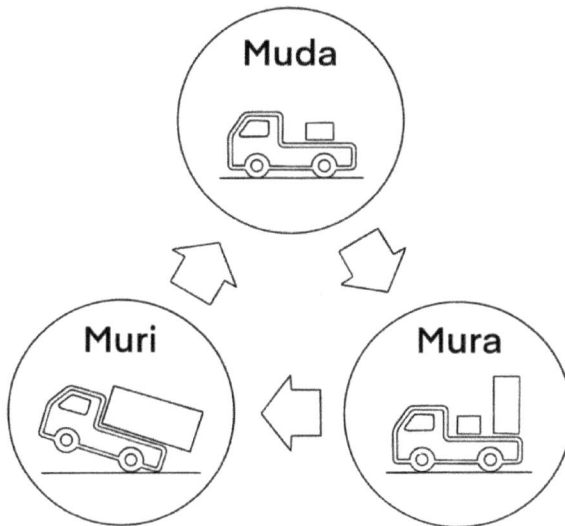

Further readings:

James Womack and Daniel Jones, *Lean Thinking*, Revised Edition, Free Press, 2003

John Bicheno and Matthias Holweg, *The Lean Toolbox*, Revised Sixth Edition, PICSIE, 2024

Purpose

Purpose defines the organisation's main objective or desired outcome. It's a key starting point to guide team efforts and decision-making towards the most critical, impactful work. Defining and staying focused on the Purpose helps to avoid waste and ensure that the team's work aligns with the organisation's overall strategy and values.

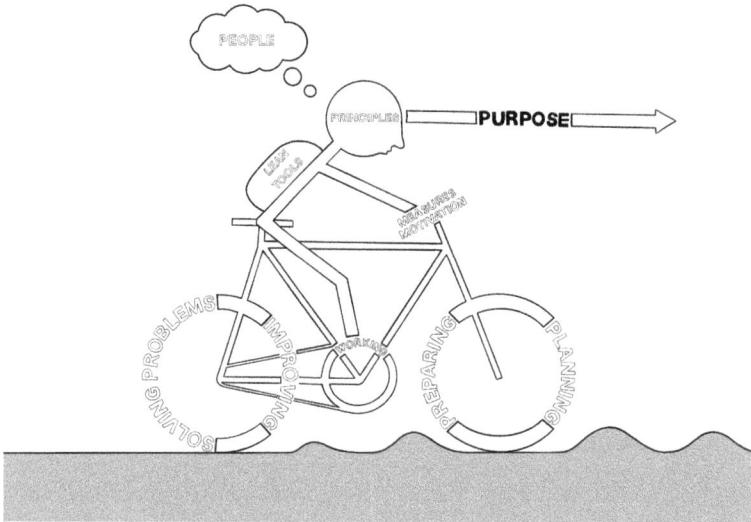

To begin, in analysing and improving a system using Lean or Agile, it is vital to clarify the Purpose.

What do you (or the organisation or system you are looking at) want to achieve? As has been said, if you don't know where you are going, then any path will get you there.

It's the same in life: Are we drifting from day to day or living consistently knowing where we are going?

In the Bicycle framework you see purpose in the direction the cyclist is looking. The cyclist knows where to go and for what reasons. This is strategy and purpose. Whilst scanning the horizon the cyclist steers the bike, making necessary adjustments along the way.

Purpose focusses on being clear about:

- What is our contribution to the well-being of others? Every successful business makes a contribution to others. If it doesn't, it will fail.
- What are we ultimately trying to achieve? Profit is one measure of contribution.

For an organisation, on a higher level, you may hear about their 'Mission'.

Ritz Carlton Hotels have a famous example, 'We are ladies and gentlemen serving ladies and gentlemen' (Pause for a moment and think of the implications of these powerful few words.) Developing a 'Mission' statement should ideally be a concise statement, not *too* brief like 'A Passion for Yes' or too vague like 'satisfied customers'. (How can we accurately define 'satisfied?')

However, there is much discussion of the differences between 'Mission', 'Goals', 'Aims' and Purpose. There seems to be no consensus. We do not wish to propose yet another set of definitions. Instead, we will stay with Purpose. 'Purpose' is widely used in Lean and in Agile contexts, where the importance of having a clear Purpose is stressed.

Purpose requires a lot of careful thought. A start may be 'The reason for this process is to...' For internal processes, instead of 'purpose', Amazon uses a 'Press Release' to communicate and clarify. This is not released to the public but is for internal use. It announces, in a few brief sentences, the anticipated final product working back from the customer's requirement, and why it is important. - try Googling Amazon's 'Press Release'.

An effective Purpose is inspiring for all involved and shows a clearly committed choice. It shows the clear difference compared to others in your field and describes where you add value and achieve results.

In Marketing there is the concept of USP – the Unique Selling Point. What unique feature induces a customer to select your product over others? A USP is quite closely related to Purpose, except that USP relates to a product whereas Purpose relates to a process.

You can think that a Purpose describes that if a process disappears today, how the world would be a different place. Would customers and suppliers be able to find a substitute easily?

Having read this you may think that a statement of Purpose is only something that only top management is concerned with. Wrong! ALL department managers and team leaders should set out their own specific statement of Purpose. Later in the book you will read about Policy Deployment (also known as Hoshin Kanri). A manager's or team leader's statement of Purpose should be derived from Policy Deployment. To repeat, a Purpose statement should not be about money or productivity but should be about customer benefits and what the manager expects from employees - and, in the best cases, what employees can expect from the manager. It is a great help to team members to be clear on aims and expectations, instead of just unstated ideas and 'muddling through'.

'Values' is what we believe in and how we behave; 'Purpose' is why we exist and what we offer to the world.

Further readings:

John Bicheno and Matthias Holweg, *The Lean Toolbox, Revised Sixth edition*, PICSIE Books, 2024, Chapters 1 and 2

Engaged People

The critical enabling factor in Lean and Agile

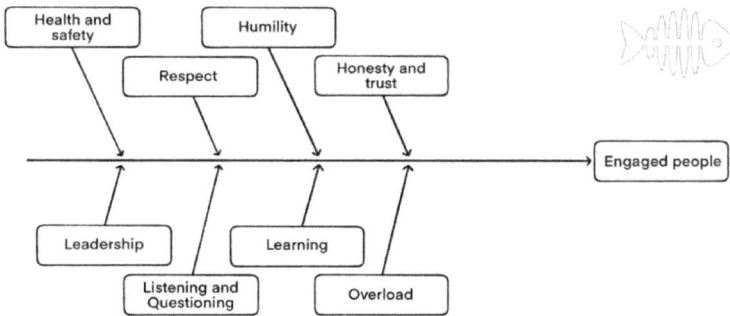

People are the critical enabling factor in Lean and Agile. How we think, feel, and behave, has a huge impact on the people we interact with. This affects the way others think, feel and behave in response. Understanding what internal and external factors, both psychologically and behaviourally, are present in that process is essential to ensuring the best possible outcome for all involved.

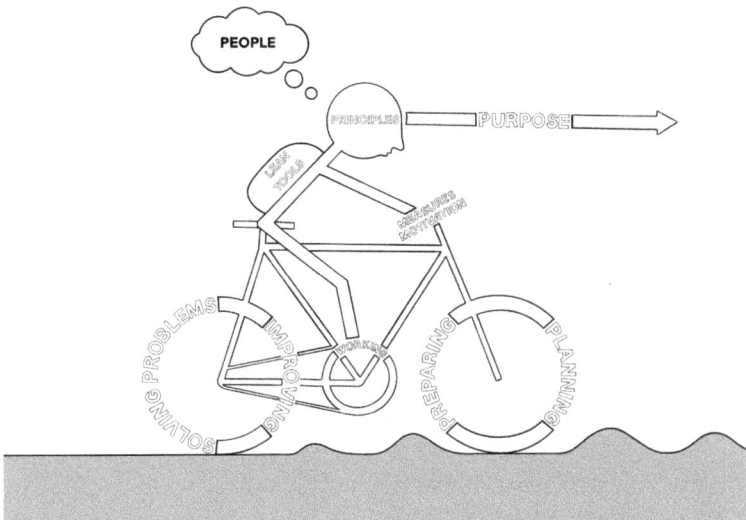

Having greater awareness of ourselves as people, how we process information and how we understand what we are feeling can shape the actions and behaviours that follow.

Health and Safety

Health and Safety, also known as Occupational Health and Safety, is a basic requirement and priority. Health and Safety involves preventing workplace harm and promoting wellbeing by following relevant legislation and actively engaging employees.

A safe working environment is fundamental for engaged people. Key elements of Health and Safety include:

- **Ergonomic requirements.** This term is used for things related to efficiency and comfort, such as chair adjustment and comfort, and adequate lighting. It extends to clear signage, workstation layout including easy to reach controls, and hot and sharp surfaces. Beyond this, it includes considerations such as lifting and bending standards, clearly marked pathways and forklift truck movements, noise levels and air quality. Acceptable working hours and shifts is an important consideration. What can assist in improving ergonomics is Anthropometrics, which is the study of human proportions.
- **Heinrich's Safety Pyramid.** This model highlights the relationship between minor incidents and severe accidents. The categories escalate upwards in severity from Unsafe Acts, Near Misses, Minor Injuries, Lost time Injuries, ultimately to Death or Serious Injury. Some organisations have strict reporting of occurrences at each level to try to get to root causes before they escalate up the triangle.
- **Attention to accident prevention.** There is the widely accepted 5 levels of control:
  1. PPE: some work conditions require personal protective equipment (PPE),
  2. Administrative controls: for example, safety training,

3. Engineering controls: for example, safety barriers,
4. Substitution: for example, less toxic paint,
5. Elimination: for example, by design. The best!

- **Health considerations.** Including medical testing and location of first aid.
- **Legislation.** Most countries have their own Health and Safety at Work legislation.

See for Yourself

Your home is a very dangerous place! We guess you have probably used PPE in the form of oven gloves or something similar. But have you ever cut yourself, burnt yourself, slipped, hurt your back, had an electric shock, collided with furniture, or fallen downstairs? Look at some of the considerations above and see how they can help. Perhaps think about some of the incidents you've experienced yourself and list these incidents under the headings of the Safety Pyramid. Then consider how to reduce the risk of each.

Respect

Respect in work situations means recognising employees' contributions, encouraging open communication and everyone treating each other with basic decency.

We respect friends and people who show ability, appreciation, and are polite towards us. Whilst we may not agree with everything they say, and are quite prepared to discuss issues, we don't resort to shouting or even violence. We expect the same behaviour from people towards us.

A good starting point to understanding Respect is the 'Foundations for Good Relations' used in TWI Job Relations. TWI is 'Training Within Industry' and is described in the Chapter on Preparing. A general statement from TWI Job Relations is 'People must be treated as individuals'. Too often, people in organisations are treated as a collection of 'resources' instead of as individuals. Building on TWI Job Relations, there would seem to be five dimensions to the meaning and practice of Respect. All five are necessary. They are:

1. Trust.
2. Appreciation. Give recognition where and when it is due. A simple 'thank you' is very powerful.
3. Ability. A recognition of a person's skills. Awareness and, even better, use of work and non-work-related skills. Find out about these and you may be surprised. By contrast, not being aware of skills, ignoring skills, sending people to courses and conferences and then showing no interest, is de-motivating and disrespectful as well as being a huge waste.
4. Psychological safety. This is also discussed in several places throughout this book.
5. Civility. Striving to understand people's viewpoints – not only about work but about personal concerns. Avoiding rudeness and sarcasm. Personal conduct and ignoring a person. In some cultures, not acknowledging a person's presence is an insult! And of course, sensitivity towards age, sex, race, religion is fundamental.

Humility

Humility refers to a leader's willingness to learn, acknowledge limitations, and value others' knowledge and experience, characterized by a lack of arrogance and ego.

It is a leader's humility which makes him or her receptive to learning new skills and ways of managing people. Ego, on the other hand is a barrier to true learning. Arrogance is the opposite of humility. If a 'leader' believes that he already has all the desired skills, knowledge and experience, learning stops and 'them and us' grows.

From a Lean perspective, leaders display **humility** by recognising that they can learn from all employees, regardless of their position on the organisation chart. There are always things to learn, simply because front-line employees are closer to the action, so their opinions are sought and valued.

In a similar vein, humble leaders are relentless in the pursuit of improvement. They actively benchmark both inside and outside of their industry.

Edgar Schein, in his essential book, 'Humble Inquiry', points out three types of humility:

1. Humility that we feel around elders and dignitaries,
2. Humility that we feel in the presence of those who awe us with their achievements,
3. 'Here and now humility' that results from being dependent on someone else to accomplish a task. It is this third type, according to Schein, 'that is the key to Humble Inquiry and to the building of positive relationships'.

For this to be possible, there are three requirements, according to Schein:

1. Do less talking,
2. Do more asking,
3. Do a better job of listening and acknowledging.

It is particularly the second one (humble asking) that is often neglected.

Humility is such as important concept in Lean and Agile that mention will be made of it in many sections of this book – for example in leadership, in listening and learning, in problem solving, in psychological safety.

See For Yourself

We have probably all met 'know-all' people! We all seem to get on better with friends who downplay their status or achievements. Try this one: Some extroverts have opinions that are worth listening to; others not. Likewise, so do introverts, although their opinions may often not be expressed so obviously. So, construct a 2x2 matrix: extroverts and introverts along one axis; ideas you consider good and not so good along the other axis. Now, fill in each of the 4 segments with people you know or have heard on TV or other media. Which category do you like best?

Further readings:

Edgar Schein, *Humble Inquiry*, Berrett-Koehler, 2013

Honesty and Trust

Trust is being honest and consistent with **Honesty.**

Honesty and Trust are prerequisites not only for Lean and Agile success, but in life in general.

Would you be prepared to deal with people you don't trust? Or people who hide information and don't share ideas for their own gain?

Deming proposed 14 Points (see later), the first of which is 'Constancy of Purpose'. 'Lip service' and hypocrisy will always undermine.

No modern organisation can control all of the actions of its employees. We live in a Volatile, Uncertain, Complex, and Ambiguous (VUCA) world, and as a result, flexibility is a must. So, people need to be trusted to respond appropriately to changing circumstances. Building trust involves sharing relevant information. The TWI guideline (see the Chapter on Preparing) is 'Tell people in advance about changes that will affect them'.

The results of a study by van Dun (see next section) confirms just how important it is for Lean leaders to establish trust with individual employees and to build a psychologically safe environment where they become active participants in continuous improvement. The authors have seen many well-resourced Lean programs fail simply because consideration of its impact on the employees concerned hadn't been thought through.

When Toyota made the decision to start manufacturing in the US, one of the big challenges they faced was transitioning American leaders who were conditioned to operate in a Command and Control environment towards a Lean Leadership style. Toyota began working in a joint venture with General Motors (GM). The GM plant was the worst performing GM plant in North America with huge problems in defects and absenteeism. Within two years Toyota had converted the plant to the best performing in North America *with the same workforce*. A supreme example of trust!

Key to this was appointing individual Japanese trainers who were quietly observing and assessing leaders (at all levels) in the background. Interventions were always in the form of questions. For example: 'What was the rationale behind that decision?', 'Who did you develop today?', 'What did you learn today?', 'Given the opportunity, what would you do differently?'. Trainers would often let the leader fail on purpose for the leader to learn a valuable lesson. The Japanese trainers also emphasised the need for leaders to view their subordinates as individuals rather than workers, for example knowing about personal difficulties. Making this personal connection is essential to building mutual trust and respect.

In many organisations tribal knowledge (pertaining to a particular group) is a big problem. Many employees see this knowledge as power and guard it closely as something which may advance their career in the future. Contrast this with Toyota where to advance your career, you must work as a team, share your ideas and develop your subordinates. It's all a question of trust.

See For Yourself

Some organisations make statements such as 'Our employees are our best resource'. This is certainly powerful, if true. Talk to your friends and family about their experiences. If this were true, how would it be apparent in their attitude to their work, and the stories that they tell?

Further readings:

W. Edwards Deming, *Out of the Crisis*, MIT, Center for Advanced Educational Services, 1986.

John Bicheno and Noel Hennessey, *Human Lean*, PICSIE Books, 2022

Leadership

Leadership (according to Peter F. Drucker) is the process of influencing others to understand and agree about what needs to be done and how to do it, and the process of facilitating individual and collective efforts to accomplish shared objectives.

Leadership is a huge topic. Sometimes it seems there are as many books and articles on leadership as there are leaders! So what follows is only a small selection of our favourite comments, that are felt to be particularly relevant to Lean and Agile.

In fact, all the sections in this Chapter relate to Lean Leadership.

In a study to identify the values and behaviours of successful Lean leaders, van Dun found that they focused their efforts on building a relationship with the person being led, rather than the actual task itself. Examples of this relations-oriented behaviour include:

- **Active listening:** *Paraphrasing to show understanding, using nonverbal cues which show understanding such as nodding, eye contact.*
- **Agreeing:** *"Exactly, I see where you are going with this".*

- **Encouraging:** *"Brilliant progress, I can start to see some results already".*
- **Giving positive feedback:** *"I like you're the way you're thinking".*
- **Co-operating:** *"This is an area where I have some experience, let's make time to look at it together".*
- **Socialising:** *"Any vacation plans for the summer, I've promised the family I'll bring them to Disneyland, if they pass their exams".*

Amy Edmondson of Harvard Business School suggests that leaders should begin by encouraging their people to become more curious, passionate, and empathic. Curiosity motivates and stimulates people to learn, solve problems and innovate at work. Passion adds meaning and a greater sense of purpose that drives effort and builds momentum. Empathy allows people to understand and appreciate other people's perspectives. Her advice for leaders is to model these behaviours and get into the habit of asking sincere questions that will elicit important insights into why people hold competing viewpoints.

Phil Rosenzweig in his stimulating and provocative book, The Halo Effect, discusses Nine 'Delusions'. For each Rosenzweig amusingly illustrates instances where the delusion is found to be false.

First, the Halo Effect itself is the tendency to see all good and no evil in a leader or organisation. For example, Toyota: a superb organisation, and a Lean icon, but also has its share of failures which, for some who hold it in such high regard, may subconsciously overlook.

Such failures of high performing organisations always elicit a 'but' response to somehow justify the failure. Of course, this is confirmation bias, the problem being that defensiveness or blindness can lead to a failure to learn. The truly great company and leader acknowledges failures and seeks to improve.

A great drawback of believing in the leadership abilities of individuals is the fundamental attribution error. Here the characteristics of the leader are overvalued whilst the influence of the situation is undervalued. So, there is widespread belief that most problems can ultimately be solved by leadership or have, at their root, a failure in leadership.

Other delusions include:

- 'The wrong end of the stick' – a focused strategy causes results but could results cause a focused strategy to be identified. What about failures of focused strategies?
- Absolute performance is attributed to the leader but may simply be the result of favourable circumstances.
- Single explanations: results are the outcome of numerous factors, but a single factor (or leader) is given credit, or blame.
- Lasting success: almost all high performing companies suffer periods of relatively moderate results, but the leader is given the blame. (Football teams almost always end up firing the manager).

See For Yourself

Try this discussion with your friends and colleagues:

- What are the characteristics of a good leader?
- Are Leaders born or developed?
- How important is it to have a leader – at work, in a sports team, in a family?
- Do you think there is such a thing as a self-directed team?
- Should leadership be top down or bottom-up?
- Is a leader essential if change is required?
- Should critical information be shared by a leader?

Do you have a leader you admire? Someone famous or someone around you? What do you admire about him/her? What can you learn from this?

Are you a leader? Do you want to be? How do others see you?

Further readings:

Bob Emiliani, *Lean behaviors,* Management Decision, Vol. 36, No. 9, pp. 615–631, 1998

Phil Rosenzweig, *The Halo Effect:... and the eight other business delusions that deceive managers*, Simon and Schuster, 2014

B.M. Bass, *Leadership and performance beyond expectations*, New York: Free Press, 1985

Desirée van Dun, Jeff N. Hicks and Celeste P.M. Wilderom, *Values and behaviors of effective Lean managers: Mixed-methods exploratory research*, European Management Journal, 35, No. 2, 174-186, 2017

Amy Edmondson, *Fixing a Weak Safety Culture in General Motors*, Harvard Business Review, March 2014

Francis Frei and Anne Morris, Unleashed*, The unapologetic Leader's Guide to Empowering Everyone around you*, Harvard Business School Press, 2020

Jeffrey Liker and Gary Convis, *The Toyota Way to Lean Leadership*, McGraw Hill, 2012

Steven J. Spear and Courtney Purrington, Jack Smith (A), *Career Launch at Toyota*, Harvard Case Study, 2004

Peter F. Drucker, *The Practice of Management*, Harper & Brothers, 1954.

Listening and Questioning

Listening is perceiving and interpreting sound to comprehend meaning. Effective listening is crucial for communication, learning, and relationships.

It is simply polite to listen to the views of others. Good ideas are not the preserve of elders or people in high positions. Beware of the HIPPO (the HIghest Paid Personal Opinion).

Richard Mullender, retired British Police Officer and hostage negotiator from The Listening Institute: *"Good listening is not 'nodding your head and eye contact.' A good listener is always looking for facts, emotions, and indications of values. In negotiations, the aim is to ascertain what the other side is trying to achieve. When you talk, you are not listening."*

Listening is the first stage for change. Listen and understand first, and only then decide an appropriate change or persuasion strategy – rational, emotional, hard or soft.

In Steven Covey's 7 Habits of Highly Effective People, the 5th habit is "Seek first to understand, then to be understood". A powerful play on words, but the sequence of communication is very clear.

A pre-requisite to effective listening, is 'rapport'. Rapport is a sense of harmony and mutual connection between people or members of a group. According to Joseph O'Connor, rapport and empathy help to create 'an atmosphere of trust, confidence and participation, within which people can respond freely'. If these three elements are missing, there won't be a great deal to listen to...

Rapport can be created to enhance the potential for openness by 'matching and mirroring body language and tonality'. O'Connor continues by saying that 'rapport is the total context around the verbal message. If the meaning of the communication is the response it elicits, gaining rapport is the ability to elicit responses.' It is these responses that should be 'heard'.

So, for us to effectively listen, 'how' we listen is critical. Whilst 'listening' is an internal cognitive function, we can demonstrate it effectively externally in how we behave, and how we respond.

Questioning involves asking open-ended questions that probe the underlying issues without blaming or criticising. Avoid closed or aggressive queries. Questioning is needed for all teams to promote transparency and collaboration.

Let us begin with a quote from Michael Marquardt in *Leading with Questions:*

"I thought a managers' job was to provide answers, to provide solutions... But I came to realize how disempowering this is, and how much more effective I could be by posing the question back to the person with the problem... It is much more effective to provide the opportunity for them to solve their own problems."

Warren Berger in *A More Beautiful Question* points out that, increasingly, answers are less important than questions. Many answers are to be found on the internet, in data bases, libraries, with experts, and with your people if you can only ask the right question. It was not always like this, but many managers still have the outdated mindset that, somehow, they must have all the answers. Schools, unfortunately, remain bastions of uni-directional instruction, and re-gurgitation during tests. That won't do in a Lean and changing environment.

Poor Questions are *Closed* or *Aggressive*. For instance:

- Why are you behind schedule?
- Why? (asked aggressively or without listening to the answers)
- Who is not keeping up?
- Don't you know the rules? (or Don't you know better?)

Or any question that is asked to illustrate the cleverness or superiority of the asker.

Challenging questions involve going to the workplace and asking, with humility:

- How do you do this work?
- How do you know that you are doing it correctly?
- How do you know that the outcome is defect free?
- What do you do if you have a problem?

See For Yourself

When you feel it is appropriate to speak, check with the other person about what they have just said. For instance, 'So as I understand it, what you are saying is...' Let the other person know that you are listening, not just by nodding, but by summarising, recapping, paraphrasing, and commenting – briefly. Try to avoid damaging rapport in these responses by saying something in some way that negatively impacts trust, confidence, or participation. Of course, not at the cost of your integrity.

Also, avoid distractions, especially visual distractions. Matching eye contact is critical to rapport and effective listening. Switch off your phone... Many people don't give full attention. Rather, they are always mentally preparing their own story, response, argument, or rebuttal. Ask yourself... Are you really listening? Or are you just waiting to speak?

Try this on practising Questioning: Get together with a friend or friends and choose a topic of mutual interest. Sport is good (Football? Swimming? Running? Gym?). Avoid politics! And then home in on a detail...

Practice *Clarifying*, for instance:

- Please explain to me... (but be careful here to avoid sounding like an accusation)
- How so?
- What happens if....?
- Could you tell me more about that?
- Why do you think that is?

and *Process*, for instance:

- What do you think would be a better way to...?
- What's your reaction to that suggestion?

- How would that affect you (or the team)?
- Could we make this process 100% fool-proof?

and on *Solutions*, for instance:

- In this situation, what are you most pleased with and what are you least pleased with?
- What would happen then?
- What could be done about that?

Learning

Learning is the process of acquiring knowledge, understanding, skills, or capabilities.

"We define learning as the transformative process of taking in information that—when internalized and mixed with what we have experienced—changes what we know and builds on what we do. It's based on input, process, and reflection. It is what changes us." - From The New Social Learning by Tony Bingham and Marcia Conner. From our perspective, Lean, and learning go hand in hand. Without Learning there can be no effective Lean Thinking.

If we don't learn we stand still – and standing still in today's world means going backwards. There is individual learning, team learning, and organisational learning. Heathcote and Powell in The Lean Post: *"Lean is about learning. Learning to find real problems, learning to face the limits of our current knowledge in light of these problems, learning to frame the gaps as learning challenges, and finally, learning to form and share actionable solutions. As such, Lean is really about learning-to-learn."*

The late Charles Handy of London Business School says, *"To learn anything other than the stuff you find in books, you need to be able to experiment, to make mistakes, to accept feedback and to try again. It doesn't matter whether you are learning to ride a bike or starting a new career, the cycle of experiment, feedback and new experiment is always there."*

There are some pre-requisites for effective learning - Personal, and Organisational:

Personal pre-requisites – What is required from you. These are discussed in earlier sections and are Humility and Listening.

Organisational pre-requisites – What is required from your environment:

- **Single and Double Loop learning.** Chris Argyris proposed the idea of single and double loop learning. Single loop learning improves the system or solves the problem. Double loop learning asks why the problem arose in the first place. A famous example comes from the surgeon Atul Gawande: Single loop involved improving the surgical procedures for eye injuries that arose with soldiers in Iraq. Double loop asked why they arose and what could be done. It turned out that soldiers were not using the protective 'shades' because they were not 'sexy' enough. The solution? Issue redesigned glasses. The result: A dramatic fall in eye injuries.
- **TIme for reflection** (or Hansei as it is called in Lean). This can be created or built in. For example, after a kaizen event, or any improvement project, allow a reflection period for participants to think about what went right and not so right. What can be learned? And think about Sprint Retrospectives in Agile as well.
- **Toleration of mistakes.** Mistakes should not be punished – far better to regard a mistake or defect as an opportunity. 'Drive out Fear,' said Deming. At the 2020 Shakir F1 Grand Prix, the Mercedes Team made what Team Principal Toto Wolff called a 'colossal f--- up' in the pit-stop that cost George Russell victory in his first GP with Mercedes. But there was no blame. Instead, Mercedes engineer Shovlin said: *"It looked like we don't know what we are doing, but the issue all comes down to this root cause where we lost a key message at a key time. We found this smoking gun, now we just need to go through the logs of how everything was working and once we have got a complete understanding of that and*

we have filled in some of the blanks that we are not certain of at the moment, we can then find a solution in time for [the next race in] Abu Dhabi."

- **Deliberate feedback.** Without deliberate feedback, repetition is ineffective – a point made by Anders Eriksson in his book *Peak*. Eriksson gives the principles of deliberate feedback summarised here as questions:
    - o Does it push people to get outside their comfort zone and attempt to do things that are not easy for them?
    - o Does it offer immediate feedback on what can be done to improve?
    - o Have those who developed the best approach so far been identified?
    - o Is the practice and repetition designed to develop the skills of the learners? And, we should add, feedback should be specific, not general.
- **Knowledge sharing.** How is the best knowledge to be shared? We know of several companies that have a data base of ideas and best practices that is routinely updated and available to be shared using key words.
- **Formal and Informal training and coaching.** Company policies to send and sponsor staff on courses, conferences, seminars. Some have book and journal reading groups. There is the old story about 'What happens if you train a person and he leaves? Or 'What happens if you don't train and he stays?'.
- **Formal benchmarking.** Process benchmarking and Product benchmarking.
- **External visits.** Several companies send their front-line employees to visit customers.
- **Experience.** How to capture experience and how to prevent valuable experience and knowledge walking out the door when someone leaves or retires.
- **Experimentation.** The 'gold standard' today is the randomised trial, or A/B experiment. Or even better the (blind) randomised trial.

- **Machine learning.** Set a computer algorithm free and let it learn by itself. Beginning to be widely used in diagnosis, forecasting, advertising, and service. The future.

Push and Pull in Learning

Push learning is when knowledge, understanding, and capabilities are learned ahead of their required use or application. When there is evidence of this learning being complete, then the application of it can be put into practice.

Pull learning is when knowledge, understanding, and capabilities are learned as they are required or *during* application. When the body of work requires the necessary understanding, skill, or capability, then the learning continues in a progressive manner.

There is a time and a place for effective learning. As mentioned, psychological safety is a critical enabler, but so is the timely way the learning is carried out. We can think of this in two approaches, 'push learning' and 'pull learning'.

Push learning focusses on a list of learning objectives in larger blocks of work, and at times, much of the content is taught well ahead of it being required. The amount of time taken to provide this type of learning is longer, and many of the items taught, if not applied, can perish over time.

Pull learning focusses on reducing the amount of time between newly acquired competencies and their application, thus adding value in a shorter amount of time. This type of learning is often in an iterative style, using application and quite often immediate feedback from an on-the-job coach or mentor.

A learning organisation stems from a myriad of practices that are discussed throughout this book.

There is a spectrum from push to pull, as shown in the Table below. Training Within Industry and other methods recommend a Training Matrix where learners and managers can see the progression of skills acquisition. At Toyota this progression is essentially pull-based, and the complete list would take several years to work through. Many employees will never progress through the entire list simply because higher level skills are not appropriate or 'pulled'.

It is not the case that push is bad and pull is good. In Lean there is a strong tendency to favour pull, but some push education can open wider perspectives. As an example, one of the authors was with an ex-student (now a consultant) in a welding fabrication shop. Due to their prior learning and capabilities, the consultant immediately recognised that the sequence of welds was like the classic Operations Research 'Travelling Salesman' problem. Using this and further analysis, subsequent implementation eliminated a bottleneck, saved the purchase of another machine, and resulted in significant additional throughput. None of the company managers, many of whom had years of experience in Lean, realised the opportunity. The moral of the story: You can't pull detail on concepts you don't know about!

Type	Examples	Comment
Push to Pull	• Classroom-only: Six Sigma theory and Lean theory. • Lean course with applications • Books • Video-based courses • Conferences • Video with interaction • Leader standard work • TWI • Problem-based learning • Kaizen events • Coaching • Mentoring • Action-learning • A3	Inefficient and wasteful. But some necessary for wider appreciation. Theory-based. More effective, but a risk of not being aware of wider possibilities. More expensive. Problem-based.

The Importance of Being Heard

Humans are not good listeners. Our brains are energy consuming machines, and as a result, they have evolved to be as energy efficient as possible. They tend to quickly filter out any information that is considered irrelevant from what we need to navigate the world. This means we are at constant risk of being influenced by where we subconsciously want to navigate towards... We see what we want to see, and we hear what we want to hear. This is the confirmation bias that we all have.

This experience is not new to us. It is easily overlooked until after the fact, and then quite often ends in a mistake, or an apology.

Maybe a friend or colleague hasn't done something they were supposed to do. Perhaps they haven't completed a piece of work, or not attended a meeting. You hear people talk about them being lazy, passive, or disinterested. It's easy to hear all of this and create a similar opinion. But by having the awareness that such bias exists, having the humility to accept there may be a different perspective, and by listening with patience and warmth you come to discover the real reason for all of this is that they were just afraid of criticism.

Only when we really understand how to listen, can we really learn from the people and situations around us. It can take more time and more energy, but this investment can prove to be invaluable not only by avoiding catastrophic errors, but by leading to greater engagement, trust, and unlocked potential.

See For Yourself

Let's do an experiment: make a day all about listening. Listen to what people have to say. Try not to judge or have an opinion about it. Just listen.

- At the end of the day reflect. What was different? Did you hear more?

- Was it difficult not to express your thoughts today?
- Would you do a day like this again?

Further readings:

Teresa Amabile and Steven Kramer, *The Progress Principle*, Harvard Business School, 2011

Anders Eriksson, *Peak*, Bodley Head, 2016

David Garvin, *Learning in Action*, Harvard, 2000

L.M. Gilbreth, *The Psychology of Management*, New York, 1921

John Bicheno and Noel Hennessey, *Human Lean*, PICSIE Books, 2022

Overload

In an earlier Chapter you heard about Muda, Muri, and Mura.

Overload is Muri. It is stress or overload in a person, but may also apply to machines and schedules.

You may have noticed people who become flustered, confused, even angry as a result of stressful circumstances. If you are given too much work you may well be unable to get a good balance in your life. Others, like your friends and family, will notice. If you have too many things 'on the go' you may forget or delay tidying up your desk.

As long ago as 1908, the Yerkes-Dodson law, as it became known, proposed a relationship between performance and 'arousal'. This is an arch-shaped parabola, with performance falling off below and above a certain level. Above a certain level the pressure of work leads to errors and work skipping. Below the optimal level workers slow down, lose concentration, and again become more careless. Decision making suffers at high workload and at low workload. Moreover, later research summarised by Neiss, suggests that with complex tasks the optimal level of workload shifts downwards. In other words, in complex tasks work 'overload' begins at a lower level. Neiss notes that the effect has been widely observed.

The Goldilocks Effect is named after the Children's fairy tale. Goldilocks comes across three pots of porridge in the bear's house. One is too hot, one is too small, one is just right. An easy-to-understand concept but with important implications. 'Goldilocks' has been used in many fields – medicine, biology, economics and psychology. Playing sport against a beginner or against an Olympic winner is not much fun, but is fun when the opposition is 'just right'.

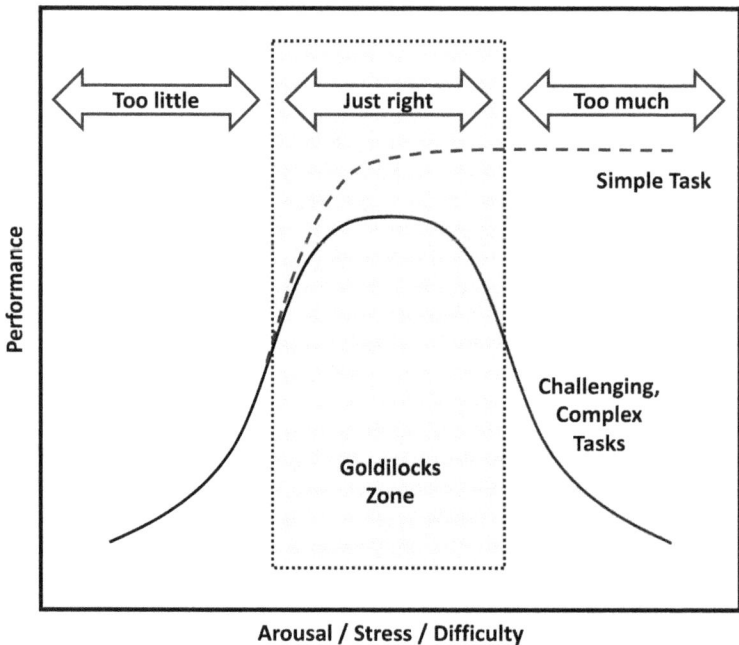

Arousal / Stress / Difficulty

Henry Ford, back in 1926, caused managerial dismay when he adopted a 40-hour work week – five days of 8 hours, against six days of 12 hours. But the outcome was an increase in productivity and a decrease in worker turnover. Many studies have since been undertaken concerning increases in workload.

Typically there is a short-term gain in output, but a long-term decline. Unfortunately, some managers gain recognition and bonus from the short-term results, leaving successors to pick up the pieces. Overload also cuts down the possibility for improvement.

The Toyota system works well because, amongst other things, overcapacity or effective overcapacity is built in with time buffers between shifts, a low worker to team leader ratio, and balancing lines to perhaps 90% of takt time. (See later Chapters). Kaizen could not be practiced with excessive time pressures. Time is needed to listen. Of course, some notable companies deliberately encourage extra time. Google famously allowed 20% of time to tackle 'what if' questions, and W. L. Gore allows 10% of time for independent projects and does not have job titles. The hugely successful on-line retailer Zappos does not have work standards for their call center operators who are expected to stay on a call for as long as it takes.

Many of us will have personal experience of overload. Perhaps you are writing a report or doing a project and run out of time. The result is less than satisfactory. Perhaps you have periods of overload at home. What happens? Your desk or room becomes untidy?

Further readings:

John Bicheno and Noel Hennessey, *Human Lean*, PICSIE, 2022

Jeffrey Liker and David Meier, *Toyota Talent*, McGraw Hill, 2007

Jeffrey Liker and Michael Hoseus, *Toyota Culture*, McGraw Hill, 2008

Finally, all lead to Engaged People

Engagement is a term used to describe to what level someone is emotionally, mentally, and behaviourally connected to their participation in an activity.

High levels of engagement show itself in how passionate, satisfied, purpose driven, and energetic people are towards their role and contribution. Generally, it is the employers and leaders that are responsible for maintaining and improving engagement levels in an organisation.

Engagement should not be optional. Numerous studies (by Gallup and by academics) have shown that employees who have a greater positive outlook and wellbeing at work are more productive, more engaged, more creative, and healthier. This is just too good to miss!

So why is this relevant for Lean and Agile? Well, research (for example by Hennessey) has identified a significant link between involvement in continuous improvement activity and employee engagement through a process of social exchange. This exchange is demonstrated through a mutual sense of loyalty, trust, and a desire to reciprocate for favours. There is a concept called 'the norm of reciprocity' which implies that exchange cannot be one-sided. An old adage is 'If you scratch my back, I will scratch your back'.

Hennessey found four Lean 'enablers' for Employee Engagement:

1. **Leader support.** This generates feelings of trust, loyalty, and a sense of obligation.
2. **Improvement in daily work**, where decisions and responsibilities are delegated to the employee.
3. **Employee recognition** that is received for work and ideas.
4. **Personal development of employees**, particularly those engaged in highly standardised work.

There are two key points to remember on the path to increasing engagement, especially when linked to Continuous Improvement.

Delegation of authority is required. Leaders need to be comfortable with this and commit to it. Delegating minor or inconsequential decision-making (fake delegation) is not the approach to take. Likewise, continuity is required. If employees are suddenly not involved or not heard see engagement levels will drop, and scepticism begins.

Rapid Mass Engagement (RME)

Rapid Mass Engagement (RME) is a non-conventional approach to culture change and employee engagement. 'Rapid' and 'Mass' are used because a short period is involved during which all (not just some!) employees are consulted in creating their own behavioural standards that are expected from managers and from each other.

Frank Devine of Accelerated Improvement has had considerable success with his Rapid Mass Engagement (RME) and the related Cathedral Model for Lean culture development.

Throughout the RME process employees are involved in adult-to-adult conversations and make decisions about behaviour at work. Employees never 'ask management' or 'make representations' about participation and engagement. As a result, employees are not the passive recipients of 'engagement' - rather they help to design their system of work in such a way that they become actively engaged. In this sense, management doesn't engage employees; management creates a process for employees to become engaged. RME is therefore a radical alternative to the traditional top-down approach to engagement and enablement.

Am I engaged?

How has work been going lately? Perhaps there is a class or project you are part of. How involved are you in what is happening? Do you feel that your contribution matters? Can you see what the end result is meant to be? Have you been asked to make decisions to shape the end result?

Are you really asked your opinion, or are you just asked questions to check your understanding? Sometimes discussing and challenging helps to change the direction of the activity or project. Do you feel heard, and do you see signs that you are having an impact? How are you spoken to? As an equal or as someone with less authority or status? Are you really involved in this or are you just following instructions from people above you?

Discussing ideas and approaches should be well received... is this the case? Is this activity something you think about and get excited, or something that just must be done?

Feeling engaged is a sense of caring about what you are doing and the outcome of your actions, both individually and collectively. 'We' are doing something exciting, and 'I' feel an important part of what we are trying to do.

See For Yourself

Do you feel engaged about your what you are currently doing? In your work or in your free time? If not, why not? If not, can you change it?

Further readings:

Tracey and Ernie Richardson, *The Toyota Engagement Equation*, McGraw Hill, 2017

Frank Devine, *Rapid Mass Engagement*, McGraw Hill, 2023

John Bicheno and Noel Hennessey, *Human Lean*, PICSIE Books, 2022

Planning

How to get things done

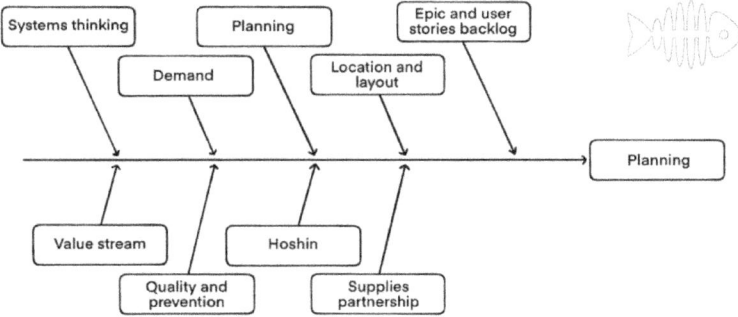

Imagine you and a friend were to go for a bike ride. Not just any bike ride, but something perhaps a bit more challenging. Maybe somewhere significantly further than normal, more difficult terrain, or perhaps your specific destination isn't totally clear at this stage. It would be reckless to begin such a journey without adequately thinking ahead.

To do this it might be wise to ask yourself a few questions prior to setting off.

- What is expected of us and how best can we manage that?
- Do we have a general direction in mind, and how will we know if we're heading towards it?
- What items will we need and where will we get them from?
- How can we make sure we know what is involved in this entire journey, whilst working effectively together?

The answers to these questions are critical to the success of what will follow.

As with our bike ride, our Lean and Agile journey begins with Planning ...

Remember, throughout this Chapter, if people help to plan the battle, they will be far less likely to battle the plan.

Systems Thinking

Systems thinking is a way of viewing and interpreting the universe as a series of interconnected hierarchies and interrelated wholes.

With Systems Thinking, you try to understand complex problems and systems by analysing the interconnectedness and dynamics of the different parts of the system. The aim is to get a view of how the different parts work together and how changes in one part of the system can affect the other parts. Systems Thinking helps you find effective solutions and predict and understand the impact of changes in the system.

Systems Thinking seeks to keep the 'big picture' in mind. 'Seeks' because this is not easy or obvious. We seek not to sub-optimise. For example, a new machine in a value stream that runs faster may be counter-productive if it leads to a build-up of inventory and an increase in lead-time. Try to consider the end-to-end value stream rather than an individual process.

Boundaries between the different elements of the system are an important consideration. Many organisations (and universities!) are organised into functional departments like Finance, Human Resources, and Marketing. But that is not how customers experience the organisation since they deal with several functions in a 'package deal'. Lean tries to look at the end-to-end value stream.

The value stream also contains several stakeholders each with different interests. We should constantly be trying to put ourself into the shoes of customers, workers, suppliers, the public and, not least, the environment.

It is important to know that being part of a system means that a change in one part may have results that effect other parts. And these results may have both beneficiaries and victims. You should act for the good of the system not just one individual stakeholder because everything you do has the potential to affect everything else.

Feedback loops are an important feature of Systems Thinking. One example: A company was experiencing increased demand which led to delivery failures. The response was to increase capacity by reducing maintenance time. In the short term there was improvement, but soon capacity declined due to repeat machine breakdowns. This led to further delivery shortfalls. This was an act in isolation, with short term benefit, that the system as a whole ultimately paid the price.

In Six Sigma, there is a useful acronym: **SIPOC** (Suppliers, Inputs, Process, Outputs, Customers). Here the process is the system. Listing all the customers and all the customer types is good Systems Thinking. Likewise, listing all the inputs to and outputs from the process encourages a more wholistic approach.

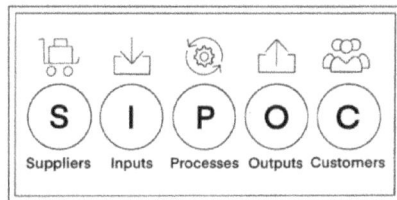

Think of football as a system!

Think of football. You can even think of your favourite player. Often debating which player is the best and why he or she can play well is only a partial viewpoint. Ultimately it is the team as a whole that is most important, not the individual players. There may be a star striker that gets all the goals and the headlines, but they would be useless without the team working together to eventually feed the ball through to them right when it counts.

Moreover, the football team is influenced by the coach, the club support staff, the fans and supporters. They all play their part in success or failure. All these groups together make up the system, and all parts of the system need to be aligned with a common purpose. When play is in progress, it is the interactions between players that make for success or failure. So, planning for successful 'team' performance requires consideration of all the parts, right down to the detail – the cost of a season ticket, players compensation, the schedule of matches – and of course, how to deal with the opposition!

Likewise, there are many other systems – a hospital, a university, or any particular organisation. Nothing operates in isolation; they are made up of a complex network of interconnected elements operating much like an ecosystem. In an ecosystem, all the components (vegetation, animals, birds, water and rainfall) are necessary. Take one component, or subcomponent, away and the whole system risks collapse.

'The whole is more than the sum of the parts.' Studying oxygen and hydrogen separately will not help you to understand water.

This leads onto the next element, which is closely associated with Systems Thinking….

See for yourself

What systems are you in? Think family, sports club, job etc.

Select one a system or process. Now try a SIPOC (Suppliers, Inputs, Process, Outputs, Customers). List all the suppliers and customer groups. Then list the inputs and the outputs. Are there any conflicts or contradictions?

- Can you see how those systems work?
- Who has which role in that system?
- And what role do you have in this system?

Value Stream

A **Value Stream** is the sequence of processes all the way from raw material to final customer, or from product concept to market launch.

By thinking in terms of a stream instead of a single stage helps to eliminate waste, optimise processes, and improve efficiency and effectiveness.

Lean and Agile uses the concept of a Value Stream. Instead of vertical silos or departments, a Value Stream seeks a horizontal view of everything involved. All the stages, from order to delivery, or request to completion, or the customer's overall experience, are mapped step by step visually. It is called a Value Stream because all the stages together contribute to customer value. This reinforces Lean and Agile viewpoint of 'customer first'. A Value Stream Map documents and shows the steps, activities, and interactions involved in creating value for customers or stakeholders, from initial demand to final delivery or consumption. The process of Value Stream Mapping is discussed in the Chapter on Improving.

A Value Stream map is drawn, end-to-end, across all the stages. This enables the identification of both value-adding steps and non-value-adding steps. As such, it is often a first step towards improvement and gives a visual representation of where to focus improvement activity.

How value is flowing through a university

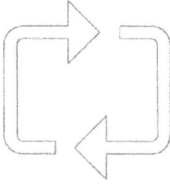

In any organisation, you can look at Value Streams to visualise how customers get what they ask for. In a university, for example, you can look at the education value stream that focuses on delivering education to students. How are curricula developed, how are classes taught, how are students assessed and guided in their studies? Which people and departments in a university have a role in this? How do they perform their tasks and how do they work together? Does this always go right the first time? And how much time does it take? Perhaps some activities are excessive? It would be helpful if staff had visibility of what other staff were communicating to students, as well as having common expectations of students.

Many of us experience problems because the organisation has done a less than satisfactory job in co-ordinating the various departments, or silos. If you complain, sometimes staff blame one another! This doesn't help at all and only leads to further frustration. Worse, if you work in a silo organisation, you may have experienced jealousy, petty comments, or interdepartmental politics.

See For Yourself

Can you make your own Value Stream? Choose a simple process from your own life. For example, getting coffee at a coffeehouse.

What steps are in this process and how do they connect? What is the waiting time and the time that your requirements are actually being met? What is the value of each of the steps in the process? Are there any bottlenecks? Can you improve this process?

Demand

> **Demand** is the needs, wants, or requirements placed on an organisation by the customer for products or services.

The amount and type of demand helps to guide decision making regarding production, pricing, and marketing. The ability of an organisation to effectively understand and satisfy customer demand will ultimately impact revenue, customer loyalty, and overall competitiveness.

Lean and Agile aims to understand demand fully so it can be matched with resources. Ideally demand can be 'smoothed' so it's more manageable, but demand may be seasonal or 'lumpy'. To understand demand is not just a question of using a good statistical forecasting package but effectively anticipating special circumstances, like weather or an upcoming sporting event, that would cause a sudden surge, or drop in demand. Sometimes, demand can be smoothed by, for example, talking to customers, adjusting pricing and marketing, avoiding large production runs, and demand management techniques. For instance, do you try to avoid rush hour delays by starting out early or late?

There are sometimes ways in which demand can be smoothed, for instance by well-timed pricing and promotional activity. Quantity discounts may smooth demand or amplify demand. End-of-month invoicing or orders may unsmooth demand. Customer knowledge is vital. Much of this requires coordination between operations, marketing, and finance. So, increasingly organisations use 'Sales and Operations Planning' meetings to achieve this aim.

Queues result from unsmoothed demand. If demand cannot be smoothed there are only three ways to cope: capacity, inventory, or time (or a combination of these). For example, in a hospital, unsmoothed demand can be met by providing more doctors (or technology), by pre-preparation of medicines, or by asking patients to wait. This is often a trade-off decision. Sometimes one of the three may not be available. For instance, a fire service cannot 'inventory' fires so faces a trade-off between providing more capacity (fire-engines?) or delaying the response time.

Failure demand is an interesting type of self-generated demand. It is the extra work created when an organization fails to do something right the first time, causing the customer to make additional contact to resolve the issue. It may constitute a significant proportion of total demand, but it is pure waste and should be monitored and the causes eliminated.

Internally, failure demand results from rework – where products or services must be re-done before completion. This leads onto the next section on Quality and Prevention.

Why would we need a fridge?

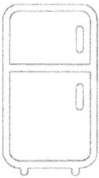

We all do a bit of forecasting demand. Buying food is a good example. Do you plan your meals for the week and then buy only what you need? Do you buy your food in bulk once per month, or do you do a weekly shop, or a daily shop? Buying smaller, more regular quantities has advantages for storage and for cash flow - you may not even need a fridge! Buying this way means that spoilage is reduced, and food, as well as money isn't wasted.

By contrast, you may have to have a special freezer if you do a monthly shop. To do this you'll need a reasonable idea of what is required, and in some way, you'll have to make a forecast for the month. However, your forecasts are also likely sometimes to be incorrect, resulting in excess or shortages of food. This causes a waste of spoiled food, or the waste of running around in a panic when a shortage occurs.

Of course, there is the advantage of a bigger shop in that you go less frequently to the supermarket, saving travel and time. It is all a bit of a trade-off. The cost and convenience of the freezer against the cost and time for more frequent shops. But if your shop was very close by, travel and time would not be a big consideration and you could afford to make more impulsive (some may say erratic!) buying decisions. As fun as this is, managing demand in this way means you will have to keep a closer eye on your accounts.

See For Yourself

Queueing is the result of unsmoothed arrival variation. We all experience queueing almost every day. Let's use queuing in a supermarket before you can pay for your groceries. Think of ways in which queueing can be reduced.

- What queueing occurs in your organisation? Orders? Deliveries? Approvals? Call centre? Software completions? Can this queueing (or delay) be reduced? What are the specific trade-offs?
- Write down the demand you see for yourself for your next holiday.
- Does it change if you go a weekend or three weeks?
- Does it change if you go someplace else?

Quality and Prevention

Quality is the series of standards or expectations that an organisation is expected to consistently conform to.

Quality affects almost every element of an organisation's decision making and performance. In planning it involves customer requirements, design, and specification. In production it involves the understanding of complexity as well as appreciating variation and process capability. Quality enables the detection and prevention of defects and mistakes, which enhances the ability to consistently meet standards and customer expectations.

Quality is a big deal in Lean, second only to Health and Safety. Quality is a huge topic in itself with entire books written on it. Many of the sections in the various Fishbone diagrams in this book are relevant, in part or in whole, to Quality. To work on quality, various methodologies are applied. Think, for example, of Six Sigma and Total Quality Management (TQM).

Prevention is the forward-thinking process of proactively preventing defects or waste before they happen. It's a proactive method to enhance the whole organisation's productivity and customer satisfaction.

'Quality is free' was a famous statement by the Quality guru Phil Crosby. What he meant was that putting effort into defect prevention would more than pay for itself. It is important to work with suppliers to ensure First Time Right (FTR) deliveries of products or services. Prevention is aided by failsafe devices (called 'poka yoke' in Japanese) such as 100% automatic weighing or automated visual inspection. Machine capability (called the 'capability index') aims to ensure that a machine is capable of producing products to the required specification. Preventive maintenance of equipment is important in maintaining its ability to produce to the correct quality standards. In the next Chapter we will look more closely at Maintenance.

If a quality problem arises at work, highlighting it as soon as possible and not being afraid to report it (see 'psychological safety' in the Motivating and Measuring Chapter section) is a necessity in a Lean organisation. This can be achieved by lights, a pull cord, or rapid reporting. On a bus, you press a button to request the bus to stop. No press, no stop. This is the same idea.

That's exactly how I want it!

Quality can show itself in our own actions and our own experiences with others, either in what we receive or what we promised. How often have you muttered to yourself "That's not what I asked for" when receiving something? Or "that's not what I meant to do" when carrying out your own plans and actions.

When making arrangements with people, it is a good idea to be clear about what you can and cannot expect. Quality is concerned with standards and the ability to consistently meet agreed standards between parties. Being clear on those standards with regards to what we think we can do, what we say we will do, and the expectations of the people we are dealing with represent potential 'gaps' in quality.

Quality can mean conformance to a specification (doing what the marketeers say it will do, or what the designers or engineers require) or satisfying customer requirements. These are not necessarily the same thing and may lead to more mutterings "That's not good enough" and "that's not what you promised".

Prevention is better than cure, which is why we check the 'use by' date on ingredients before we start cooking. Likewise, checking oil, water, tyres on your car or motorbike will help you to avoid a nasty surprise and expense.

We all make mistakes due to all sorts of reasons – being in a hurry, not following instructions, being distracted, reading a label incorrectly, or simply being careless. Or you may make a mistake with your partner or friends for all sorts of reasons – from not listening to simply forgetting or not thinking. Can these be prevented? This is often difficult, but there are some forms of assistance available. For example, a notification on your phone, a warning sound in the kitchen, or a safety jar that is difficult for children to open.

Making bold promises not in line with capabilities, not agreeing standards and expectations, not being proactive about prevention, and simply not checking the right thing at the right time are all prime suspects for the cause of poor quality.

See For Yourself

Which quality standards do you have when you buy groceries? Do you have different standards for (let's say) buying furniture? Which ones are the same? And what makes then different?

Hoshin

Hoshin (or Hoshin Kanri, or Policy Deployment) is a planning and management methodology that aligns an organisation's goals, resources, and processes to achieve breakthrough improvements and long-term success.

Hoshin is frequently used in Lean organisations for planning, and for communicating the plans. The term "Hoshin" is derived from two Japanese words: "hoshin", meaning "compass" or "direction," and "kanri", meaning "management" or "control".

Hoshin is a participative methodology. Instead of targets and policies being simply imposed from above, Hoshin seek to gain buy-in with inter-function consultation. This is known as **'Catchball'** after netball whereby the ball is passed between players in a team before being thrown over the net. This also encourages Systems Thinking. The process takes longer than just giving top-down orders, but as a result, implementation is invariably more successful due to the greater levels of consultation and consideration. What is an important feature of the Catchball process is that it takes place over several levels.

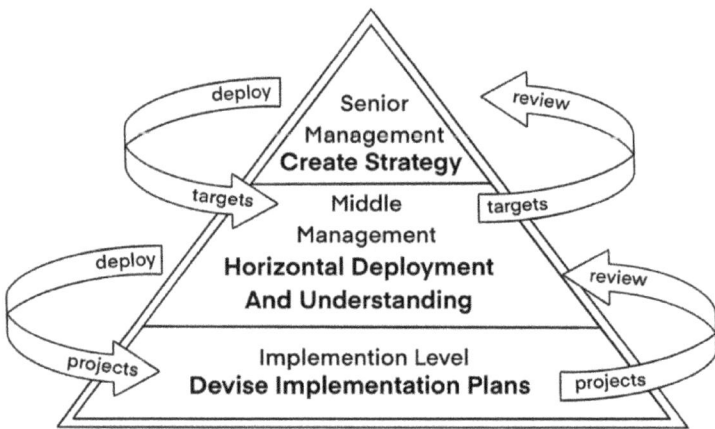

A common technique for Hoshin is the use of an 'X Matrix'. This is a tool that aligns Strategic Priorities, Targets, Projects and Responsibilities across departments, teams or sections, visually representing the strategic planning process, promoting Value Stream Thinking, and tracking progress for better alignment and performance. One example is shown in the figure, but several organisations develop their own version.

Notice that this is a value stream or systems approach with interconnections between Strategies, Targets and Projects and requiring actions from a range of departments.

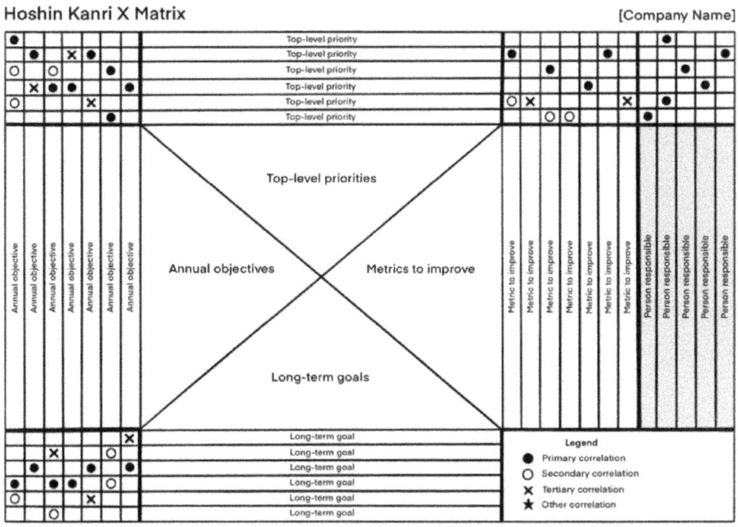
Hoshin Kanri X Matrix
[Company Name]
Top-level priority
Top-level priority
Top-level priority
Top-level priority
Top-level priority
Top-level priority
Top-level priorities
Annual objectives
Metrics to improve
Long-term goals
Annual objective
Metric to improve
Person responsible
Long-term goal
Long-term goal
Long-term goal
Long-term goal
Long-term goal
Long-term goal
Legend
Primary correlation
Secondary correlation
Tertiary correlation
Other correlation

What to do now if I want to be rich in 3 years?

How do you translate your longer-term aims into daily activities? Of course, your chances depend on real talent, developed skills or insights you have. By working hard on those, your chances are much higher. Do you have a plan, or do you just take every day as it comes? Are you pro-active or re-active?

Many self-help books have been written on these and related questions. A famous example is Stephen Covey's '7 Habits of Highly Effective People'.

Perhaps you have longer term aims already? An amount you'd like to save? A weight loss target? Perhaps completing a study programme or significant physical activity? Whatever these larger aims are, they need to be focused and prioritised.

The ability to break these large activities in to measurable and realistic smaller objectives set over time is the key to turning them into reality. Doing this also relies on reviewing how well you're doing against them - there's always an opportunity for improvement!

Whilst some of these targets may be personal, some may impact a wider network such as your friends, your family, or the team you're a part of. Regardless, both directly and indirectly, their help is vital. So clearly sharing your aims will massively assist in gaining their support, or at worst, avoiding any conflicts in what you and the people around you are trying to achieve.

Beyond this, the focus is on consistency and forming the correct habits. Done well, this will ensure one objective after another is achieved, ultimately realising your longer-term aim.

In summary, clear objectives, measurement, and consistency is the key. The "Working" Fishbone will help.

See For Yourself

Can you make a Hoshin Matrix for yourself using the example above? Begin with your long-term strategic aims. Then develop the aims for next year. Then develop the projects for next year that will lead to the aims being achieved. Then, break down the projects into your regular activities (perhaps diet, sleep, study, money, holidays, friends, transport?). Look at the implications of the projects for each of these activities. Finally, can you suggest measures for each of the activities?)

- You can now take his one step further by 'deploying' your Matrix into a next level of detail. For instance, your first level projects become your detailed strategic objectives, and these are broken down into sub-projects, and the sub-projects into detailed activities.

- Perhaps you have another example you want to explore. Develop a Hoshin Matrix for your football team?

Location and Layout

Location refers to where exactly the most suitable location is for our key activities to take place.

Layout refers to the most efficient way items and equipment are 'laid out' or placed physically.

Location and layout decisions are critical but sometimes missed or forgotten about. These decisions have long term implications for cost, waste, and competitiveness. A facility with poor layout can simply not be Lean.

Location involves tough decisions that are influenced by costs, labour availability, tax and other incentives, energy, transport and proximity to suppliers and customers, and building regulations. History, sentiment, and weather may also play a part. Some progressive organisations actually give staff a say in location decisions. Retail location decisions are absolutely critical, as you can imagine. Supermarket layout is an area of considerable expertise. And web site layout can make or break an organisation.

In a factory, placing a large machine, perhaps a press embedded in concrete, or perhaps the location of storage facilities, can influence the waste of transport for years. Poor layout and its impact often tends to creep up over time as the product line or demand changes. An answer to the poor layout problem is a 'Spaghetti Diagram' which is often an early step towards a Lean factory, hospital or office. A Spaghetti Diagram is a visual tool that illustrates the physical flow of materials, equipment, or people in a facility, highlighting inefficiencies, bottlenecks, and opportunities for process improvement, leading to increased efficiency and better performance.

A good approach is to allow operators themselves to experiment with layout. Encourage them to participate in ergonomic and movement considerations. This not only taps into their process experience and expertise, but is very important for buy-in and sustainment of changes. Participation is a strong motivator.

One possibility is to use flexible workstations that allow adjustments to be made until the work stabilises. Throughout all of this, of course, health and safety are paramount.

Location and Layout: The importance of Cells

Cells are important aspect in Lean. Instead of layout being arranged by similar machines grouped together, a cell is laid out according to the process steps. Process workstations are located close to each other. Often, a cell is laid out in a U shape, which allows operators to move easily between processes. A U shape also aids visual management, feedback, and team working. Line balancing (distributing workload, evenly across a process) is also made easier.

The big advantage of a cell is a dramatic reduction in lead time. Instead of batches being moved between separated processes, one-piece-flow between closely situated processes is made possible.

Sleeping in the kitchen?

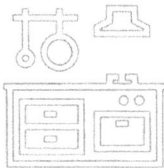

Everyone has Location and Layout considerations. For example: where will you live?

Often this involves a series of decisions – which country, which city, which area? Then of course, will it be a house or apartment? Within the house then comes layout. Again, a series of decisions need to be made.

Which room will be the kitchen, the bedroom, and so on. Within each room you have the furniture choice and its arrangement. And then there is storage and lighting to think about.

Often, trial and error is involved to get a 'feel' and the function of the room. People find that an arrangement needs changing. Perhaps the family has grown or maybe people have moved out. Some other points to consider:

- Many Layout decisions should be delegated. Children get to arrange the layout in their own rooms.
- Ergonomics is involved. How comfortable and effective is something to use? Are cupboards within easy reach? Door handles in the right place? Is the lighting sufficient? Computer screen at the correct height?
- Safety considerations. Install smoke detectors? Handrails for stairs? Medicines and knives out of reach of small children?
- In the kitchen, minimise walking and bending. Aim for a logical layout based on function– for example, is the bread next to the toaster? Tea next to the kettle? Sink near the dishwasher? Perhaps also minimise temptation by keeping sweets and snacks out of sight...

See For Yourself

Which layout improvements can you make in your own house? Think about convenience or safety or maybe you have another reason. Who do you have to involve to make these changes?

Supplier Partnership

Supplier Partnership refers to working closely with existing suppliers in a way that is mutually beneficial and sustainable.

Like all partnerships, this involves clear communication and sharing information about future requirements, as well as sharing risks, rewards, and opportunities for improvement. Trust is essential to a supplier partnership, and for the mutual benefits to be realised, collaboration needs to be planned strategically.

A Lean or Agile operation requires suppliers that are honest, dependable, of good quality, and that supply at reasonable cost. A Lean operation would like to avoid checking incoming supplies if possible. Ideally, supplies arrive just when they should – 'just in time' not too early or too late for what they are required for. This is also called 'on time in full' or OTIF.

Moreover, Lean suppliers would be practising Lean themselves so that their costs would be under control and perhaps reduce with time. The benefits of reduced costs are shared between supplier and manufacturer. Some manufacturers send their staff to help suppliers improve their productivity. Increasingly, suppliers both to manufacturers and to service organisations, are judged on their environmental responsibilities and on the way they treat their employees. And sometimes it would be good if there was co-operation with a supplier on design and specification – to their mutual benefit. To achieve all this would be the aim of partnership supply.

In choosing suppliers a Lean manufacturer would look not just at cost, but also at quality, dependability and the potential to co-operate and to make improvements.

Supplier partnership does not just happen. As mentioned, it must be based on mutual trust with perceived advantages for both supplier and customer. It takes time and patience to develop. As the supplier gains confidence about future contracts and their certainty, it is encouraged to invest in its own performance and capabilities. Ultimately, the customer benefits from good quality and dependable supply. Perhaps a supplier could be given assistance with their Lean implementation as an additional benefit of the partnership. This can be done, for example, by helping them achieve regular level schedules and lower inventory.

By contrast, if a supplier is always uncertain about future contracts and experiences varying demands, and the customer is uncertain about quality and delivery, the Lean programmes of both parties will suffer.

What is your preferred supplier?

Generally, we prefer to use suppliers that we personally know. These may be shops and restaurants or trusted tradespeople. We prefer to use these suppliers because we are confident in the products or services they supply based on our experiences with them. We know we can get exactly what we require because we are in personal contact, and we know that their prices will be fair and honest.

Because of this contact we can also share tips and even make requests. These often help the supplier improve and be more successful. These suppliers are often local and their reputation is therefore very important to them. As a result, repeat custom is mutually beneficial.

Other suppliers we may use regularly, and although we don't know them personally, they are dependable and honest. We trust them. Examples of these are utility suppliers and e-commerce companies such as Amazon. Often these regular suppliers are paid automatically by direct debit which of course saves us time and is more convenient.

There are also other suppliers we don't really know. Sometimes they provide a good service, but not always.

So, although we have different categories of suppliers - trust and convenience play a big role in how we select and interact with them.

See for yourself

Think about everything you eat in a week. Which suppliers do you have? Which one do you use frequently?

- Do you select suppliers on cost alone? What other considerations should be relevant?
- And are there suppliers you hardly use or maybe just once?

- Can you make a list of reasons why you return to suppliers that you use frequently?
- Can you think of ways in which a regular supplier could improve? (For example, in price, convenience or layout?)

Epics and User Stories Backlog

Epics and User Stories Backlog are Agile concepts that help manage and prioritise high-level requirements and user stories, breaking them down into smaller, manageable pieces for efficient development, collaboration, and continuous improvement.

An Epic is a large, high-level user requirement or feature, usually a significant piece of functionality (what the 'thing' actually does) or a set of related features that can be broken down into smaller, more manageable pieces called user stories. Epics help to provide an overall vision and direction for the product development and are written from the user's perspective, using the format: "As a [user role], I want [feature] so that [benefit]". For example: "As a Healthcare Professional, I want a Patient Management System so that I can efficiently manage patient data, schedule appointments, and track treatment plans."

The User Stories Backlog is a collection of user stories that describe specific requirements or features from the perspective of the end-user. User stories are short, simple, and written in a standard format, such as "As a [user role], I want [feature] so that [benefit]." User stories help to break down Epics into smaller, more manageable pieces (or specific activities) and prioritize them for development. For example: "As a Healthcare Professional, I want to be able to view patient medical records so that I can access important information when treating patients."

By using Epics and User Stories Backlog, Agile teams can focus on delivering value to the end-users, adapt to changing requirements, and efficiently manage the development process. They promote collaboration, transparency, and continuous improvement, leading to better product quality and customer satisfaction.

A party for my 20th birthday

Every once in a while, you might want to celebrate your birthday with a bigger 'splash' than usual. For example, on your 20th. But how do you do it? That's your Epic. It requires a plan and preparation. It helps to cut everything that needs to be done into small pieces and then tackle them in a planned way.

When are you going to throw the party? And how about that football match that weekend? What about your best friend's wedding the next day?

And music? Will there be a DJ or a band? Or just put together a nice playlist. Maybe better no music at all...

Who will you invite? Will you keep it small and just for intimates? Or rather finally invite everyone you've wanted to meet up with for so long.

And what about food and drinks? Will it be fancy or casual?

All things to think about, all User Stories. Put them together on a list, your Backlog, and make sure you know what comes first and when you need to have what done. Then it will be a really fun party!

See For Yourself

Let's say you want a new house. What would your Epic look like? "As a [user role], I want [feature] so that [benefit]."

- What User Stories do you see to break this Epic in smaller parts?
- Maybe you can make the Backlog?
- You will notice some similarities with Hoshin. Hoshin uses Strategic aims, One year aims, Projects, Activities and measures. How do these line up with Epics?

Further readings:

John Bicheno and Matthias Holweg, *The Lean Toolbox, Revised Sixth edition*, PICSIE Books, 2024, Chapters 13, 19

John Bicheno and Philip Catherwood, *Six Sigma and the Quality Toolbox*, PICSIE Books, 2005

Martin Hinckley, *Make No Mistake*, CRC, 2001

For a wonderful book on statistics in Quality, see Don Wheeler, *Understanding Variation*, SPC Press, 2000

Amy Edmondson, *The Right Kind of Wrong*, Cornerstone, 2023, has extensive sections on mistakes and errors at work – good and bad types. It is the right kind of wrong if you can learn from the event.

Preparing

How to make sure you are ready to perform?

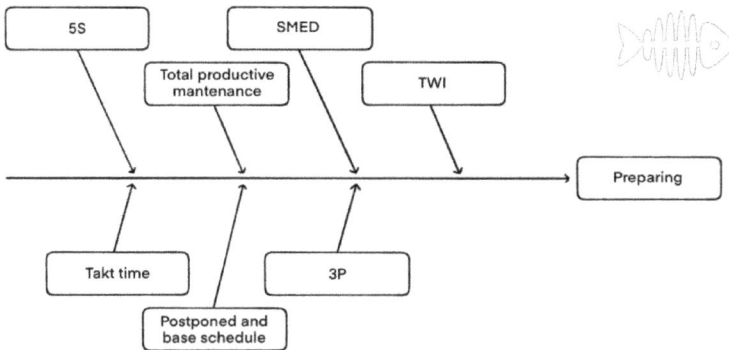

That bike trip...

With the planning complete, we need to prepare for action. Planning is concerned with the longer term and as such dictates what we need to be prepared for. But how to prepare is a different question.

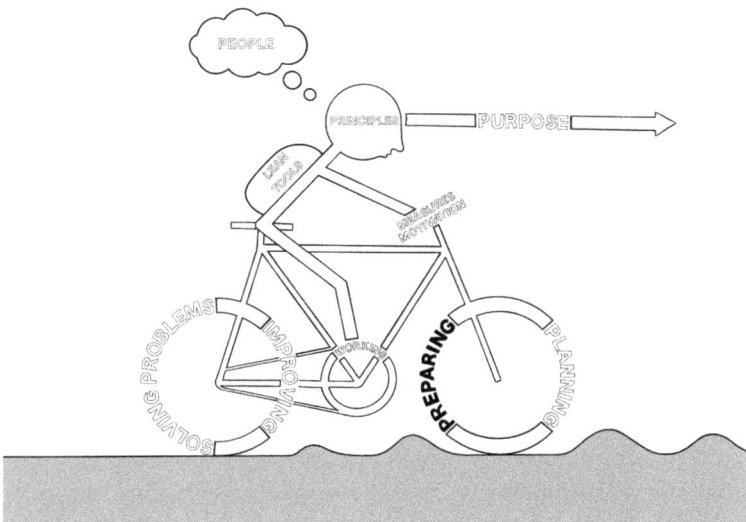

Preparing aims to find the most suitable means of dealing with what is ahead, by being organised, equipped, and ready.

So given the length, terrain and duration of our bike ride, certain factors need to be prepared for.

What average speed will we cycle at? How often should we stop to discuss our progress? How can I ensure I keep the bike in safe working order? What tools will I need? Where and how will I store them? If I have to change a tire how quickly can this be done? How quickly can I learn or teach others about the skills needed to do these sorts of tasks correctly?

Preparing is critical to effective and responsive performance.

To help us best prepare, Lean and Agile provides us with some very useful solutions.

5S

5S is a tool consisting of 5 progressive steps aimed at an organised, standardised, and safe work environment.

The results of good 5S are waste reduction, variation reduction, and productivity improvement at the workplace. 5S also influences operator attitudes; from working in a chaotic, messy environment, to working in a spotless, safe environment. 5S isn't limited to the shop floor environment and certainly applies in the office.

5S applies to people, to workstations, to service, to computer file arrangement, to suppliers, and to the environment. 5S can also be applied to information and communication preparation.

The classic 5S's are: **S**eiri, **S**eiton, **S**eiso, **S**eiketsu, **S**hitsuke. Most commonly these are translated into **S**ort, **S**implify, **S**can, **S**tandardise, **S**ustain, but many other synonymous terms have been used. Often, a sixth S -for Safety – is added. A good idea!

We all probably make use of 5S (or at least 2S) even though we may not realise it. For example, perhaps you use a 'shadow board' for your tools, keep knives and forks in specific slots, or use folders in your computer to organise files.

So 5S is an ongoing, stepped procedure. It is simple to follow and to teach to others, and its results have immediate visual impact.

1. First **S**ort and throw out all unnecessary items (or locate infrequently used items away from the workplace).
2. Then **S**implify – cut duplication and arrange in the most appropriate locations.
3. **S**can means being on the lookout for inappropriate items, files, signs, things not working as they should, even strange noise.
4. **S**tandardise (or stabilize) is sometimes the missing step – It is important to develop standards following on from the first three steps.
5. **S**ustain means keeping the procedures going – perhaps with audits – but certainly by making everyone aware of 5S responsibilities.

Tidy at work is tidy in your head

Do you find yourself regularly having to search for items you know for sure you had recently, you just can't seem to remember where you put it last? How many times have you 'lost your phone' or 'can't find your keys', or perhaps lost a file you're certain you saved? If it is a solid 'yes' to any of these questions you're not alone! We all, to some extent, have the same problem on a daily, and often frequent, basis. It doesn't always take hours to find and recover them, but these often-small amounts of time, collectively add up. The fact that it is small yet often, means we don't realise how much cumulative time is being lost.

Despite these issues representing time loss and elements of frustration, there may also be safety issues – such as tripping over items left on the floor, or not having critical items when desperately needed. Perhaps, we hope not for you, items in the wrong place can lead to arguments.

We all seem to work better in a tidy environment. It enhances quality of life. Our day-to-day actions seem to flow seamlessly from one to another when we have clarity, and consistency in our immediate environment. But 'overload' as mentioned in the People section may lead you to temporarily ignore your untidy desk.

See For Yourself

Can you apply the 5S to your workplace. What happens when you reorganize your desk, cutlery in your kitchen or toolbox. Is there a lot to sort? And how do you sustain this new situation? What do you have to plan for sustaining it? Experiment with 5S and have fun.

- Can you be obsessively tidy? There are famous cases where managers have insisted on no personal items or clear desks at the end of every day. What is your view on this?

Takt Time

Takt time is a term used for the regular, uniform rate of progression of products through all stages of a process, from raw material to customer delivery. It is the drumbeat for the flow rate of products.

Takt time originated from assembly line work. *'Complete one product every x minutes.'* This implies arranging and levelling all the stages in production to have the same takt time. Although its origins are in assembly work, takt time has been found to be a useful concept in many types of operation. For example, *'complete one stage of software development every week'*, or *'aim to serve one customer on average every 10 minutes'*. Takt helps with design of work and with establishing the correct number of employees that are needed.

The drumbeat assists in the coordination of activities along a value stream, with all activities working at or near the takt time, ensuring a smooth predictable, and stable flow of progress. Takt time is calculated by using the available work time (say per day) divided by the average demand per day.

Takt time applies not only in Lean factories but in several other environments. For example, it can apply in a hospital, in construction, in maintenance, in new product introduction, and in software development. In these cases, takt time is not a strict time but a guideline – often with a frequency in hours or even weeks.

In all these cases takt time helps with flow coordination – arranging supplies to arrive at regular intervals, work completion to be more predictable (perhaps one house completed very two weeks), monthly cash flows, and to help identify problems, where takt time is being routinely missed.

It should be noted that there are two variables – one to do with the customer (the average demand), the other to do with the manager (the available work time). Therefore, if demand changes, a manager could maintain the same takt time by adjusting the available work time. The available time is the actual time after allowances for planned stoppages (for planned maintenance, team briefings, breaks, and a little slack for contingencies). Demand is the average sales rate (including spare parts) or arrival rate of work plus any extras such as test parts and (we hope not) anticipated scrap. Takt time is expressed in time units: e.g. 60 seconds (or 60 seconds between completions).

For machines and processes, working to takt time may mean slowing down. Strangely and counter-intuitively, slowing down to achieve synchronization may lead to a reduction in lead-time. This is because queues build up at machines that run faster than the takt time. This simple realization of synchronisation, to try to get all machines in a plant running at the constant takt time, can have dramatic results. It changes the job shop into a pseudo assembly line.

Of course, knowing the takt time assists with planning and scheduling and further enhances our ability to keep potential chaos in check.

Dance to the rhythm of the beat

Oscar Wilde famously stated, *"Without order nothing can exist – without chaos nothing can evolve"*. Even in the most progressive, original and iconic music, sometimes almost hidden, but ever present, is the drummer providing structure, timing, and order. Likewise, in an orchestra, the conductor coordinates timing amongst all sections. No-one tries to go faster or slower than the beat dictated by the flick of their wrist. Without a drummer or a conductor, there would be no order, and chaos would be allowed to progress beyond control.

See For Yourself

Think of a fast-food restaurant. Where can you identify takt time? Maybe you can spot it when you are out in the town. Can you see how they use takt times?

- Try to find 3 examples of takt time the coming week.

Total Productive Maintenance (TPM)

TPM is an equipment maintenance methodology that has a focus on prevention of breakdowns, increasing equipment effectiveness, and training and involvement in maintenance tasks.

TPM aims to eliminate the impact of unplanned machine breakdowns by involving people in taking ownership of their equipment's scheduled maintenance and repair tasks. Additionally, and significantly, TPM empowers and encourages people to proactively search for maintenance and service improvement opportunities. TPM concepts apply in factories, but also in much wider situations like vehicle maintenance, restaurants, offices, buildings and at home.

Like Total Quality, TPM is not only the concern of the maintenance people. Everyone has a role to play such as checking and reporting any abnormalities observed, cleaning equipment or simple maintenance tasks. In work situations, raising awareness is done by placing red cards on equipment, or switching on a light to indicate a maintenance issue. The 'kamishibai' board shows maintenance tasks that must be done by displaying cards— red 'to be' done'; green 'done'.

The late Peter Willmott, the UK TPM 'guru' said there are 6 aspects to TPM:

- Increase the Overall Equipment Effectiveness (OEE) or equivalent measure
- Improve existing planned maintenance systems
- Make routine front-line asset care part of the job
- Increase skills (training, team working and problem solving)
- Enable early involvement in new equipment specification.
- Make performance visible. (This last is an aspect that is often ignored.)

TPM also uses the concept of 'The Six Big Losses'. These apply, with some modification in all types of operations – factories, hospitals, service, IT, and construction. They are

- Breakdowns
- Setup and adjustment (Changing from one activity to another)
- Idling and minor stops (Think of your computer system! And interruptions.)
- Reduced speed (machine or internet provider)
- Quality losses (Scrap and rework, including editing of reports)
- Start up (at beginning of day or shift)

Measuring The Six Big Losses highlights issues and guides priority.

See For Yourself

When you wash your car or your motor bike, it is good practice to take the opportunity to check the tyres, and if applicable water, lights, screen wash. Change or top up when necessary. Prevention is always better than cure.

Likewise, everyone has (or should have) simple maintenance tasks. Cleaning your apartment, computer screen and keyboard. Changing batteries in a smoke detector. Frequent, proactive cleaning and checking, and when necessary, fixing, repairing, or replacing.

Total maintenance applies to yourself - Cleanliness and hygiene, eating healthily, medical and health checks, as well as staying functionally fit and active. Total, complete, comprehensive.

Where can you use TPM? On your car of bike as mentioned above? Or some other place like your house? Choose one item and note how can apply TPM on this item.

- Which of the Six Big Losses apply in your work or at your home?

Postponement and Base Schedule

Postponement is a supply chain strategy that involves delaying certain production or assembly steps until the last possible moment, typically just before the product is sold or distributed to the end customer.

A **Base Schedule** is a production plan that focuses on the big runners in a factory site's portfolio.

Use the 'variety in the supply chain as late as possible' concept. Do not add variety until the last possible moment. The clothing brand Benetton is a famous example with their 'jerseys in grey' concept. Jerseys (sweaters) are made all the same except for size.

This is 'push' or general forecast driven production resulting in a buffer or inventory stock. However, the colours, logos, and extras have great uncertainty so the varieties are added thereafter on a pull basis. The result is upstream stability and downstream flexibility.

Upstream, before the postponement point, there is less variation and greater stability. Design has an important role to work out where the postponement points are.

Some organisations use postponement just before the delivery stage. Perhaps the computer's configuration is delayed until this stage. Postponement is routine amongst car assemblers. A class of cars is made all the same up to the 'body-in-white' stage, but thereafter final assembly can configure literally millions of options. Of course, this helps to reduce inventory, even though buffer inventory may be held at the body-in-white stage.

Many people postpone leisure activities until the weather becomes suitable. But they might still have a plan on what to do if the weather changes. To not have a plan would risk wasting a good day!

Much evidence, for example from Ian Glenday, shows that perhaps only 6% of products account for 50% of total production volume. Further insight comes from the classification of demand patterns into *normal*, *seasonal*, *erratic*, and *lumpy* patterns. (from John Darlington). Together, these insights mean that there is almost invariably an underlying stable demand for a small proportion of products that account for a large proportion of volume. These can form a base schedule that can be made with high regularity perhaps every day. The advantages of a base schedule are enormous: high stability, repetition, low inventory, thereby facilitating other Lean activities such as training, quality, changeover reduction, and kaizen.

Postponement and Base Schedule is the very essence of Agile software development.

Postponement refers to the practice of delaying the commitment to specific details or decisions until the last responsible moment. This concept is aligned with the Agile principle of embracing change and maintaining flexibility throughout the development process.

A Base Schedule typically refers to the initial plan or timeline created at the beginning of a project. However, it's important to note that Agile methodologies recognize the likelihood of change and emphasize adaptability.

How Postponement works within the Agile framework:

- Delaying Decisions: Agile methodologies encourage teams to postpone making decisions until final commitment becomes absolutely necessary. This approach allows the team to gather more accurate and up-to-date information, reducing the risk of making premature or uninformed decisions.

- Flexibility: Postponement is closely tied to the Agile value of responding to change over following a plan. By delaying decisions, teams can remain adaptable to evolving requirements, customer feedback, or market conditions. This flexibility is crucial for delivering a product that truly meets the needs of the stakeholders.

- Last Responsible Moment: The last responsible moment is the point in time when a decision must be made to avoid negative consequences or to ensure the project progresses smoothly. Postponement encourages delaying decisions until this moment to maximize the available information and minimize the chances of making the wrong choices.

The Base Schedule in Agile is not treated as a rigid, fixed plan but rather as a starting point that will evolve as the project progresses. Agile teams work in iterative cycles, often in short increments known as sprints. After each sprint, the team reflects on the progress made, incorporates feedback, and adjusts the plan accordingly. This iterative and adaptive approach ensures that the project remains aligned with evolving priorities and requirements.

In summary, Postponement encourages delaying decisions until the last responsible moment to accommodate changing circumstances, while the Base Schedule in Agile is a flexible starting point that evolves as the project advances through sprints.

Sometimes postponement is smart!

Using a slow cooker has become popular. Here, a meal is produced ahead of time, the slow cooker is switched on, and the meal is ready when people get home from work. This saves time in the evening when people like to discuss the day's events or are in a hurry to go out. When the meal is made in the morning, no time needs to be given over to actual cooking time. Variety can be added to the meal in the evening – perhaps wine and dessert, depending on what the people feel like at that point in time.

On a holiday, you may plan where and how to go and where to stay. But you postpone decisions on what to do and what to eat each day, until the day itself.

Both these examples involve some initial commitment, but retain some flexibility due to uncertainty, or potential for greater added value at the point of consumption or use.

In your life there are some activities that you do every day – sleeping, brushing your teeth, eating breakfast and dinner, plus some personal activities. These don't always take place at exactly the same time or duration every day, but they do happen every day. These activities are usually not listed in your Calendar because they are so regular, they are fixed, routine, and consistent, but with potential for modification at the last possible moment.

See For Yourself

Let's take the holiday example from the Framework Chapter. You are going on holiday. Where is it wise to postpone and where can you apply base schedule?

- Do you have activities that you postpone when you should not postpone? Perhaps delaying writing an assignment until the last day, and then discovering that you don't have sufficient time to do a good piece of work! (This is not postponement, it is procrastination!)

SMED

SMED (Single-Minute Exchange of Die) is a manufacturing technique aimed at reducing the time it takes to changeover a production line or machine from producing one product to another.

The goal of SMED is to minimise the time a machine or process is not producing, but more importantly to allow smaller batches to be made thereby cutting lead time and inventory, and enhancing flexibility. But, importantly, changeover does not only happen in factories: it happens everywhere – from airlines to zoos, from breakfast to bedtime, from restaurants to roadworks.

The late Shigeo Shingo developed the classic changeover methodology, that was called SMED for Single Minute Exchange of Dies. This was for large press machines.

The classic Shingo methodology is:

- Identify and classify internal and external activities. Perhaps make a video? Internal activities can only be done while the machine or process is stopped. External activities are preparations that can be done before the changeover takes place.

- Separate 'internal' activities from 'external' activities. The number of external or preparation activities should be maximized. Cut or reduce waste activities such as movement, fetching tools, and filling in forms.
- Try to convert internal activities to external activities wherever possible (for example by pre-heating a die).
- Use engineering solutions on the remaining internal activities. There are many tricks, from quick release nuts to constant platform shims, to multiple hole connections done together. In service situations, you may have to redesign forms, reduce computer mouse movements, or use a different medium. Always ask if activities can be done in parallel instead of in series.
- Finally, minimize external activity time. Why? Because in small batch production there may be insufficient time to prepare for the changeover during a batch run.

Of course, the later steps can be expensive, so there is a trade-off between expense and time.

There are many further refinements, including focus on:

- **'Online activities'**: by internal and external task reallocation, or by designs that allow the sequence to be altered – for example simultaneous rather than sequential steps.
- **Adjustment**: by reducing trial and error by for example indicators and shims, or by design which allows 'snap-on' adjustment.
- **Variety**: by standardization and standard operations or by design which reduces the possibilities of variation – poka-yoke.
- **Effort**: by work simplification and preparation or by design which incorporates simplification – for example fixing multiple hoses by one fixture.

How long does it take you to get yourself ready?

A famous example of Changeover Reduction is the Formula 1 pit-stop wheel change. The methods are now so well known that 4 wheels are changed in under 3 seconds. The absolute priority is to get the car back on the track and up to full speed. A myriad of previous internal activities are now external, with many engineering solutions in place for the remaining internal activities. The results of this speak for themselves. Of course, this type of changeover involves a large team and is very expensive. Time is the priority, but changeover cost is not important.

But changeover reduction thinking can be applied in many day-to-day situations. How long does it take you to get dressed in the morning, to make breakfast, to prepare your things for work? You probably do quite a few of the quick changeover steps yourself, without thinking about it. For instance, you may set out the things for breakfast the night before, and during making breakfast you may make toast and coffee simultaneously. In these situations, costs are often negligible.

Changeover also applies in the office and in service. Every time a new piece of work is started or returned to, there is both physical and mental time lost. Several studies on multitasking have shown mental readjustment times of up to 15 minutes. This is hidden changeover waste. Whilst you're mentally "changing over" you're not adding value.

Another famous example is SouthWest Airlines that minimises the non-value time for aircraft. Aircraft are only productive whilst flying, so SouthWest aims to minimise the time an aircraft spends at the dock. Sometimes pilots and stewards assist with loading and unloading during changeover. Likewise, cruise liners have carefully worked out routines so that they can get 2000 passengers unloaded and 2000 new passengers (plus food) on board, all in less than 12 hours.

As you become sensitised to 'SMED' you will become aware of many possibilities: Road repair delays, airport security checks, university registration, changing over a table for new customers at a restaurant, seeking parking space, filling your car with fuel, searching for 'lost' keys or items, and activities in a lecture (or meeting) room before a lecture can start.

See For Yourself

Think about when you are working on getting ready in the morning. Which changeover steps do you use? How much time do you save with this? Or is it more convenient? Why is it important for you?

- Can you think of even more changeover steps to improve your life even more?
- Think of how other concepts like 5S, TPM, and visual management can assist.

3P

The '**3P**' (Production Preparation Process) is a participative methodology used to design or redesign a process layout or cell.

This should always be done for new product families, when a facility is planned, and where a process needs overhaul. Originally found in manufacturing, 3P is now appearing in office and hospital settings. Distinctive features of this are participation, alternative generation, and physical modelling. The aim is to try out and test various approaches before committing to full scale implementation. Also, of course, workers will be much happier if they work in an environment designed by themselves.

3P should always be undertaken by an open-minded, participative team of people from the area, and from any other appropriate area such as quality, engineering, design, and scheduling. The steps in a factory are as follows, but similar steps are applicable in many other work (and even home) environments:

1. Establish the aims. This may include productivity, space, defect rates, workstation reduction. Determine envisaged production rates and calculate takt time where appropriate. List the design criteria.
2. Draw a flowchart of how the product or family is currently made or envisaged. Add photos. Add 'kaizen bursts' of current problems.
3. List the function steps, not the process steps. ('Removing metal' is a function step; 'Milling metal' is a process step.) Use verb plus noun.
4. Collect the parts, material and tools for each function step. Set these out on a table for all to see.
5. Make a preliminary work balance (Yamazumi) board using takt (planned cycle time.) Return to this board and modify as work proceeds. This may involve timing various activities.
6. At this stage, some 3P exercises are split into sub teams each of which generates solutions. This is to foster a greater number of ideas and to prevent idea domination by strong personalities.
7. Generate alternatives to make or assemble the product. The classic Toyota approach is to require at least 5 ideas. Never accept only one solution! This can be done on two levels – broad concept design, and detailed steps. For instance, assembly may be done by pressing together, clipping together, screwing, welding, bolting, moulding, even 3D printing. Remember to incorporate poka-yoke, quick change over, safety, ergonomics, good material handling solutions. Quick change parts presentation is desirable for multiple products. The whole idea is a low cost, flexible solution.
8. Evaluate against the aims. Select the most appropriate solution or solutions.
9. Take the more promising ideas and construct a small-scale model. Use simple materials – cardboard, shoe boxes, toilet rolls, Lego. Use the model for 'simulation'. Consider part and operator movement. Discuss with input from various team member viewpoints. Modify and adjust.

10. Return to steps 7 or 8 until a preferred solution emerges. Return to Step 5.
11. Now build a full-scale mock up using cardboard boxes, wooden tables. Modular tubing is ideal. Get operators to move around, simulating making the product. Use a flipchart and record ideas.
12. Finally, build the actual cell, perhaps still retaining modular tubing and flip chart or ideas. Further modification is always possible.

See For Yourself

Did you notice the similarities or crossover between this section and the section on Layout? Indeed, there are similarities in the approach, and everyone is involved with Layout. Not everyone would go as far as the 3P process briefly described above! However, you could easily do a 3P exercise in your home, or office, or service situation. You can certainly try a simplified 3P with your partner if you move into a new home or install a new kitchen. Here you would probably not use takt time or Yamazumi, but experimenting with carboard boxes can be fun!

Of course, today, there are several inexpensive layout packages available for your computer. Some stores even offer this possibility for furniture or kitchens.

- Try a 3P process? Choose a situation like getting ready in the morning and let's go.
- How does it help you?
- What did you gain? Time, money, convenience? Something else?

Further readings:

Allan Coletta, *The Lean 3P Advantage*, CRC Press, 2012

Michael Baudin, *Working with Machines*, Productivity Press, 2007, and Lean Assembly, Productivity Press, 2002

TWI (Training Within Industry) (JS, JM, JR)

TWI is a hands-on approach to teaching, coaching, and learning new skills in a work-based environment.

TWI was developed during World War II in the USA to address the huge shortage of trained workers needed for war production. The focus was on the supervisor, considered to be a key person for team productivity.

A supervisor needs three team skills, in addition to technical knowledge. These are how to teach a job, how to improve a job, and how to work with people. These three were named job instruction (**JI**), job methods (**JM**), and job relations (**JR**). The three were referred to as the three-legged stool, to emphasize that all three were needed. Safety was also incorporated in all three, but later became an additional fourth type- job safety (**JS**). Each skill JI, JM, JR, and JS has four steps, thereby making learning and remembering easier. In each case the steps are learned by repeated practice under close observation.

TWI is arguably the most effective and widespread training system ever developed. It remains in force today. TWI training takes place throughout Europe, USA and Japan with Toyota remaining an enthusiastic user, although not using the classic TWI wording. The concepts of JI evolved into '*standard work*' and JM evolved into '*kaizen*'.

Today, a 'supervisor' may still be called a supervisor, but also could be called a team leader or manager.

Element 1: Job Instruction

The 4 steps are:

1. **Prepare the worker.** Put the person at ease and in the correct position.
2. **Present the operations.** Here the important process steps, key points, and reasons for the key points must first be identified and then demonstrated. This is called Job Breakdown.
3. **Try out performance.** Here the trainee demonstrates understanding by repeatedly going through the process steps, key points, and reasons for the key points. 'Continue until YOU know that THEY know'
4. **Follow up.** Check the person frequently. Encourage questions.

And always remember: 'If the worker hasn't learned, the instructor hasn't taught'!!

Some may argue that detailed Job Breakdown is not appropriate in a service context where personal interaction is required. We would argue that EVERY process has <u>key points,</u> but that slavish adherence to all process steps is often inappropriate.

Element 2: Job Methods

Job Methods is the basis of Kaizen. Although the name has changed, the essential very detailed steps remain. The four steps are:

1. Break down the current job: List all the details covering material handling, machine work, hand work.
2. Question every detail: Use why, what, where, when, how, who.
3. Develop the new job: Eliminate, combine, rearrange, simplify.
4. Apply: Get final approval, write up the new standard, give credit where due.

Element 3: Job Relations

Job Relations addresses one of the most challenging parts of a supervisor's job - establishing and maintaining good supervisor–employee relations and dealing with problems when they arise. Job Relations is aimed at giving supervisors basic skills in behaviour in organizations, motivation, and communication.

The Four 'Foundations of Good Job Relations' are 'solid gold' for every person in a management position. They are:

1. Let each worker know how he/she is getting along.
2. Give credit when due.
3. Tell people in advance about changes that will affect them.
4. Make best use of each person's ability.

The TWI four steps on JR (job relations) are:

1. Get the facts: Be sure you 'have the whole story.' Find out what rules and customs apply. Talk with the individuals concerned. Get opinions and feelings.
2. Weigh up and decide: Don't 'jump to conclusions.' Fit the facts together. Check practices and policies. What possible actions are there? – note plural 'actions' not 'action'. Consider the effect of possible actions on the individual, the group, and on production. Sometimes a period of reflection is helpful.
3. Take action: Don't 'pass the buck.' Consider if you are going to handle the problem yourself, whether you need help, and whether the actions should be referred to others. Consider the timing of the action.
4. Check the results: Did your action help? How soon and how often should you check? Watch for changes in output, attitudes, and relationships.

A TWI Job Relations mantra is 'People must be treated as individuals'.

Learning Karate

Like Kata (see the Fishbone in the Chapter on Improving) TWI has much in common with learning Karate. You learn the basic skills from an instructor. These become 'embedded' as you practice. Later you progress to application.

How do you learn to do a new job, at home or at work? Or alternatively, how would you train someone else to do a particular job you are familiar with? Every job has those particular 'key points' that are the essential steps or activities required for the job to be done to the correct standard. There are many ways to do any particular job, but there are always a few key points essential for people to know how to do a *good* job. Once we have done this, we have to ask the question, do you want to improve the job? And how do you get fellow workers (or family) to support the work being done in this way?

There is overlap between TWI JI and standard work. Learning to cook is a great example. You follow a recipe, and practice. But you will seldom become a chef unless you are instructed by an experienced chef who will point out the critical key points in making any dish.

There is the story of the New York tourist asking how to get to Carnegie Hall. 'Practice, man, practice!' is the answer! Certainly, but also practice under the guidance of a master.

See for Yourself

A great way to practise Job Instruction is to try to teach something practical to someone else.

- Try to find a short practical job that occurs with some frequency – for instance washing dishes or washing a car.
- Begin with a short job that you are absolutely familiar with. Don't attempt the exercise with an overly mental job such as

writing a piece of computer code, or with an unusual job. But note that you can also try the exercise with an activity such as a daily morning meeting.

- Write down the steps to do the job. This is the Job Breakdown sheet. Some of the steps will be 'key' – in other words steps that are critical for the success of the job. Be sure to write down the reasons for each key point. This is an essential point for understanding and remembering the job! An important part of the job might be to have the appropriate tools or materials available and laid out. (Here, note the overlap with the 5S method described in an earlier section.)

- If you select cooking as the job, you might find a recipe set out in a book. This would be useful, but many recipes will not have set out the key points and the reasons for the key points specifically. Once you have the Job Breakdown sheet you are ready to begin to instruct.

- Find the trainee. Follow the four steps as given in Element 1 above. Make sure that the trainee knows each step, the key points, and the reasons for the key points.

- Ask the trainee to speak the steps out loud as they are done. You will probably need several cycles of instruction. But, as said, 'Continue until YOU know that THEY know'.

Further readings:

John Bicheno and Matthias Holweg, *The Lean Toolbox, Revised Sixth edition*, PICSIE Books, 2024, Chapters 16 to 21

Patrick Graupp and Bob Wrona, *The TWI Workbook*, Second edition, CRC Press, 2017

Allan Coletta, *The Lean 3P Advantage*, CRC Press, 2012

Michael Baudin, *Working with Machines*, Productivity Press, 2007, and Lean Assembly, Productivity Press, 2002

Working

How to keep things going.

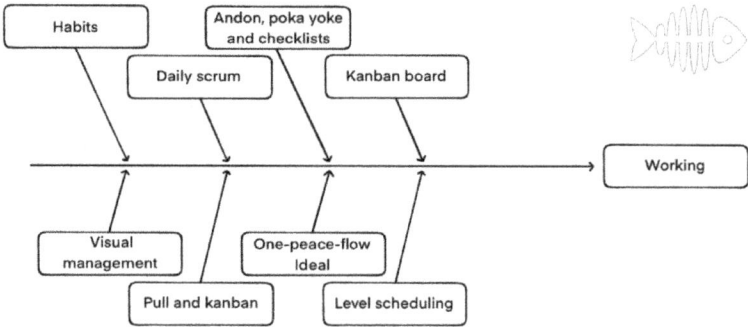

After all the planning and preparing, at some point the pedals start turning, and it is time to get to work. Once the working begins, the opportunity for issues and risk become larger – it is very problematic to have to react to significant changes once our journey has begun.

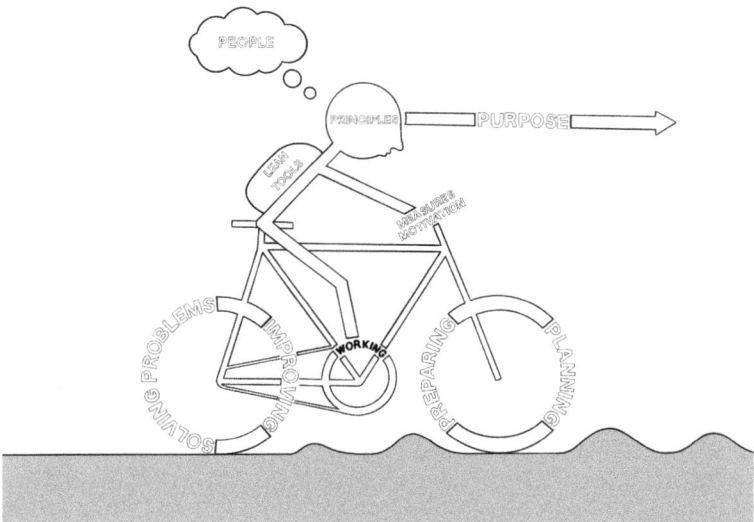

The journey is long and to work effectively whilst avoiding issues, requires constant awareness of what is happening and what is required.

Again, on our cycle trip...

- How will we all work collectively to set and keep the pace?
- How often will we get together to discuss progress and make changes? Have we agreed to stop at regular intervals to check and support?
- How will we signal to each other to speed up, slow down, or identify hazards in the road?
- In fact, how will we communicate with each other about anything? What if I have an empty water bottle, empty stomach, or empty legs!

You're not cycling alone and you won't make it alone. Lean and Agile teaches us how to work together, be responsive, and act just in time.

Once we start, we want to keep things going.

Habits

A **habit** is something we subconsciously repeatedly do.

A habit often goes unnoticed by persons exhibiting it, because a person does not need to engage in self-analysis when undertaking routine activities.

Good and productive routine activities can become habits. For example, attending a daily team meeting at the workplace, checking a particular machine every week, always asking for customer opinions. This is known as the Que, Action, Reward cycle.

A *que* might be an alarm, which triggers an automatic *action*, this leads to a *reward* – often a feeling of satisfaction. When you get in a car (que), you automatically fasten the seatbelt (action), and then feel secure for your travel (reward).

Habits work against chaos. The alternative is 'every day is a new adventure'.

Always remember that a habit is a subconscious decision triggered by an environment or situation. We do this sort of thing all the time. If we watch a movie, buy popcorn! Don't even think about it. It's your reward!

Advertisers spend huge sums linking environments with products. Again, if we watch football on TV, have a beer! It's your reward! So, with Lean, think about what situations should eventually trigger what subconscious action or decision you desire. If you log on to your computer in the morning, check daily stats, respond and be rewarded with up to the minute team information.

Maurer has pointed out that the human brain finds it easier to accept small changes than big changes. Little changes add up. It's kaizen. In Lean and Continuous Improvement, the goal of a habit is not to solve a problem, but to become a problem solver. The goal is not to improve relations with a particular team member but to become an excellent team facilitator. At home, the goal is not to cook a good meal but to become a good cook. There is much in common with Carol Dwek's mindset and her plea for a 'yet' outlook. ('I can't do mathematics YET.')

Good habits are facilitated by making them easier to do. (Pulling the Andon chord at line side), and bad habits are decreased by making them harder to do. (Removing the large batch ordering default in a production control system, or put that chocolate bar on the top shelf!)

The bottom Line on Habits for Human Lean is:

- Set up an easy-to-do Ques or Triggers: We always have a morning meeting at workplace. We always do an After-Action Review (AAR). We always use PDCA.
- Then follow through with an Action procedure: Who will be present? How will it be done? Make it easy to do. (Close by; easy to see; convenient.)

- Reward: Make the action satisfying: Show progress, share information, share encourage discussion at tea break, comment on achievement.

We are what we repeatedly do

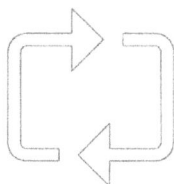

We all have habits, some good, some not so good. With time, a habit becomes automatic, like putting on a seat belt in a car or brushing your teeth. You don't debate, you just do it. That frees up a lot of your deep-thinking time. This is not becoming a 'zombie' or an 'automaton' but living more effectively.

We have 'runner, repeater, and stranger' events in our lives. With luck, our heart beats and we keep breathing (runners). We sleep every night, not always at the same time, or for the same length, but every night (repeaters). It is the repeaters that form habits. Other activities are different from day to day (strangers). Strangers can be unusual or original in type, as well as infrequent and irregular, but they are not habits and so do not benefit from the benefits of good habits.

See For Yourself

What habits do you have? Let's use your habits in having dinner in the evening. Do you know what triggers (or prompts) this habit?

- What in having dinner assists improvement, in yourself or with others?
- Have you tried to establish a habit? (Going to the gym each day? Dieting?)
- What was successful for you in doing so, and why? What did not work out, and why?

Further readings:

Carol S. Dweck, *Mindset: The New Psychology of Success*, Random House Inc, 2006

Charles Duhigg, *The Power of Habit*, Heinemann, 2012

James Clear, *Atomic Habits*, RH Books, 2018

Robert Maurer, *One Small Step Can Change Your Life: The Kaizen Way*, Workman, 2004

B. J. Fogg, *Tiny Habits*, Virgin Books, 2020

Russell Poldrack, *Hard to Break*, Princeton Univ Press, 2021

Visual Management

Visual management is a system that promotes taking actions (or deliberately not taking actions), as a result of actually seeing a physical object, indicator or sign.

The opposite is classic 'command and control' where orders or instructions are issued *verbally*. The impact of Visual Management is usually immediate or almost immediate. It does not rely or wait for formal authorisation from a person or manager. Instead, the sign or chart gives the authority.

Visual management is the grease that enables the majority of Lean concepts to work together: 5S, Muda, purpose, Kaizen, Kanban, Scheduling, Quality, Standard work, Problem solving, Value Stream Mapping, Learning, Improvement, and more. In that sense, 'visual' is a systems approach to management. And moreover, visual management is low cost – probably the greatest 'bang for the buck' of any Lean and Agile concept. Of course, visual is not about making the place look good, it is about improving performance. It assists in making the current situation instantly apparent, at a glance.

Gwendolyn Galsworth, an authority on the topic, defines a visual workplace as one that is '...*self-ordering, self-explaining, self-regulating, and self-improving; where what is supposed to happen, does happen on time, every time...because of visual devices.*'

And a '*visual device is a mechanism or thing intentionally designed to influence, guide, direct, limit or even guarantee our behaviour by making vital information available as close to the point of use as possible to anyone...who needs it without speaking a word*'. Note the word 'behaviour'.

Of course, 'visual' should also include sound and smell. Think of your car or your kitchen!

Visual management is THE way to share information – instantly!

In factories, and increasingly in offices, there is often a team display board that shows all relevant information relating to the area or cell. The board shows 'SQCDMMME' (Safety, Quality, Cost, Delivery, Maintenance, Morale, Management, and Environment). Better Lean plants display a link with the Hoshin X Matrix. In addition, many locations would include an Idea board showing the progression of any idea from suggestion, through discussion, and onto implementation. Very often, in all these, coloured magnets are used to indicate status – on track, intermediate, behind.

Also, a skills matrix (or I L U O chart) indicates achievement or advancement from beginner to instructor. Operators are shown on rows; tasks are shown in columns. ILUO are not letters, but show 4 stages of progress from one stroke 'I' to two 'L', and so on.

Galsworth says that, at every workplace, 'what do you need to know' and 'what do you need to share (to do my or the team's work)', should both be shown visually. And, of course, the person at the workplace needs to decide this – not the manager. The manager needs to decide what needs to be done, but the person at the workplace needs to decide and communicate what information is needed to do the work.

An immediate test for an organisation's Leanness or Agility is simply a brief look around. This is probably as good, if not better than, an audit that may take hours.

Galsworth uses 'six core questions':

1. Visual Where? (correct locations, as in shadow boards, footprints)
2. Visual How? (as in standardized work or single point lessons – including pictures)
3. Visual When? (tasks need to take place, as in a Heijunka box or Kamishibai board)
4. Visual What? (to be made or done, including dimensions, stages in idea boards, problems)
5. Visual Who? (as in tool or maintenance responsibility,)
6. Visual How Much? (as in Kanban or a supermarket).

All of these help cut wastes in the form of time, paperwork, errors, miscommunication as well as encouraging detection of problems and idea generation. 'A picture is worth a thousand words.'

Galsworth uses an excellent analogy to a railway crossing to illustrate four different levels of visual control:

1. Visual indicator. A warning sign. No control. (Labels on a shelf?)
2. Visual signal. Flashing lights. Some power. Lights and sound when trains approach. (Red light when a machine stops?)
3. Visual control. Automatic barriers. Significant power. (Poka-yoke?)
4. Visual guarantee. Separation of road and rail track. Absolute power. (Design that prevents misassembly?)

Of particular note is the Gemba concept (or 'Genshi Genbutsu') or 'go and see for yourself'. Of course, this is an expected part of A3 problem solving and kaizen.

'Learning to see' is the title of the most well-known book on Value Stream Mapping. Yes, indeed a good value stream map is drawn at 'the Gemba', not in the office. But learning to see goes much further: Taiichi Ohno of Toyota was said to require new managers to spend several hours in a chalk circle drawn on the factory floor, or on a chalk X, standing in one place and observing waste. Stay there until waste and variation has been noticed sufficiently well. Or, if not observed sufficiently well, 'Look more' and again 'look more', and yet again!

We should not assume that putting up a poster or sign will be interpreted as we intended. The same applies to any written piece. To ensure consistent interpretation, a better way is to test the poster by experiment. Ask questions, and when necessary, adjust. Try to avoid terms such as 'unacceptable'; instead use facts or quantifiable metrics such as 'the defects level is 5%'. 'The force is 5750Nm': This avoids the confusion and prevents people from wondering if they meant Newtons or Pounds. (Ask NASA and the European Space Agency about that one: it cost them a mission to Mars!)

Visual Management can also send out signals. No reserved car parking - don't park your Ferrari in the staff car park. *(I wish...)*

Generally, as a rule, humans are not good observers. Our brains fill in a lot of missing information for us, and we are deceived. The Dutch artist Escher's drawings are good examples of this. "Ascending and Descending" (In Dutch "De Stenen der Wijzen") is a famous 1939 work by Escher featuring an infinite staircase climbing upwards, with the stone figures following a kind of mathematical pattern. The image is drawn in a way that makes it seem like the stone figures are running in an infinite loop, but at the same time they are also arranged in perfect order.

Various Japanese words are used in this section. These will be explained in the sections that follow.

See for yourself

Throughout each day our eyes receive hundreds of visual signals and cues. Unfortunately, not all of them are valuable, some conflict, and most have varying levels of Galsworth's levels of control. But ask yourself the question, how much of your daily activity could be improved by having greater visual management and control?

How many of the six core questions are not answerable or have to be discovered due to lack of visual management? How often do things go wrong or get missed due to missed visual information?

Instantly communicating where something is, or meant to be, such as keys or a TV remote? Instantly confirming when an activity is due or done, such as a payment or appointment?

How reassuring is it to have an instant clarification on the correct and agreed standard on how activity should be completed such as a meal preparation or unfamiliar activity? How much safer and secure would things be?

Improving our daily performance can be done by looking at the activities within our day and understanding the power and impact of the visual cues and signals around them. Not only for ourselves, but the people our activities impact also.

Take a look around your workplace or your place of residence. List the visuals. Are they used? Do they conform to the idea of 'what do you need to know?' How could they be improved.

- What visuals can you see in the street? Could they be improved? For instance, consider the four levels of visual control. Is each visual matched with the appropriate level of visual control?

- Can you make your own visual?

Further readings:

Christopher Chabris and Daniel Simons, *The Invisible Gorilla: and other ways our intuition deceives us*, Harper, 2011

Amy Edmondson, *The Fearless Organisation*, Wiley, 2019

Gwendolyn Galsworth, *Work that makes sense*, Visual Lean, 2011

David Sibbet, *Visual Meetings*, Wiley, 2010

Carol Tavris and Elliot Aronson, *Mistakes were made but not by me*, Harcourt, 2007

Daily Scrum (and Daily Team Meeting)

The **Daily Scrum** is a 15-minute event for the members within the Scrum Team. Ideally it is held at the same time and same place every working day of the Sprint for focus and consistency.

The purpose of the Daily Scrum is to measure and discuss progress towards the Sprint Goal and when necessary, make relevant changes to the Sprint Backlog, adjusting the upcoming planned work.

Daily Scrums drive team communication, identify obstacles, promote quick decision-making, and consequently eliminate the need for other meetings.

Likewise, it is now common in factories and in offices to hold a Daily Meeting, usually at the beginning of the day or shift. The purpose of the Daily Meeting is the same as that of that of the Daily Scrum.

Note that some software developers now consider that a daily Scrum is wasteful and therefore only hold a Scrum meeting when needed.

Both Daily Scrum and Daily Meeting incorporate the concepts of Gemba and of Visual Management. A meeting usually begins with the team meeting at a visual board located at the Gemba. The team leader will always facilitate. Usually there will be an escalation procedure whereby, if an issue cannot be resolved at the team level, the issue is taken by the team leader to the next, and regularly scheduled, level. Here the issue will be discussed with other team leaders, in line with value stream thinking. Eventually, if still not resolved, the issue may be discussed by senior management.

Ideas for improvement are also often discussed at a Daily Scrum or Team Meeting. Here, once again, the starting point is the Idea Board.

Gathering around the hot stove

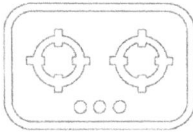

At home you are unlikely to have regular, formal family meetings. (Although some families do have them). However, many families discuss the days events (in advance and in retrospect) around mealtimes. Some families use the 'hot stove rules' even though they might never have heard of these. The analogy is as follows: A hot stove gives warmth to the family. Family members feel comfortable and are unafraid. The family gathers around, supports and discusses. Parents use constructive, loving criticism. If the stove is touched, it burns instantly. But there is no memory of a misdeed, only continuing warmth being given out.

You may receive a similar support from your student group, or from people you live with.

See four yourself

Do you have a reminder board in your kitchen? Is it used regularly – for instance before going shopping? Who makes use of it? Can anyone add to the lists?

- The same questions may apply in an office. Here, however, who is responsible for keeping the board up to date, and who leads discussion about points that are raised on the board?
- An interesting point about Daily Scrum and Daily Meeting Boards is: does the leader or facilitator start with the problems or with the achievements? Discuss the pros and cons of each.
- Many will have Calendars in their computer or mobile phone. Who, if anyone are they shared with? Should they be shared?

Further readings:

John Bicheno and Matthias Holweg, *The Lean Toolbox*, Revised Sixth edition, PICSIE Books, 2024, Chapters 8, 14, 40

Pull and Kanban

Pull is a concept that initiates workflow activity only when there is actual demand to be responded to.

Kanban is a method to visualize workflow, reduce waste, and increase flexibility by using real-time demand signals.

A pull system operates on the principle that only when items have been used, they are replaced. This is the opposite of a forecast-based system where a *prediction* leads to a response. A prediction may or may not be correct ('lucky or lousy') resulting in excess or shortage.

Due to the responsive nature of a Pull system, there is frequently an overlap between pull and visual management. Both authorise action without further authority. Pull releases work depending on system (usually inventory) status, thereby capping 'Work in Progress' (WIP) inventory to a maximum level. There are two situations: In a line or a cell, work is not released to move to the next stage operation unless that next stage is ready to work on it. This is achieved by a balanced line or by Kanban squares placed between the stages. When the square is full the previous stage stops work and only re-starts when the square becomes empty. This avoids overproduction.

A common use of kanban is in a factory. Here inventory is placed next to a workstation. When inventory is consumed and falls to a particular level a Kanban card is sent to a store or supplier to signal that more inventory is required. Kanban cards move in a loop from workstation to supplier and back to the workstation together with the required replenishment inventory. On its return journey to the workstation the Kanban card is attached to a container or box containing a batch of components.

There are a variety of Kanban types:

- Card
- E-ban
- Fax-ban
- Kanban square
- Light signal

In logistics, the Lean ideal is to have pull based demand chains, not push-based supply chains. Pull should take place at the customer's rate of demand. In demand chains this should be the final customer, not distorted by the intermediate **'bullwhip' effect**. Easier said than done!

Pull means a short-term response to the customer's rate of demand, and not over producing. Think about pull on two levels: on the macro level most organisations will have to push, by forecast, up to a certain point, known as a postponement point (think back to the Benetton example and their 'Jersey's in grey' from earlier). Pull takes place downstream from that point, responding to final customer demands. If a postponement point can be moved further upstream, dependence on forecasts is reduced. On the micro level, for instance, a pull signal is given when additional staff are needed at a supermarket checkout to avoid excessive queues.

In a later section, the use of 'kanban' in software development and in service is discussed. This other type of kanban is different to that discussed in this section.

Pulled into Action

To some, pull might mean trying to attract someone you like. Thankfully that is not what is meant in Lean. Pull essentially means working at the rate of demand, instead of pushing work forward in anticipation. The activity is literally 'pulled' from you by some form of 'trigger' ahead of you.

We often use our own 'kanban' even though we may not recognise it as such. For example, you may replace toilet rolls as they are used. Regularly used groceries are replaced when used. Your iPhone signals that its battery needs to be recharged.

The story goes that Toyota's Taiichi Ohno, when visiting America, was impressed by American supermarkets that replaced inventory on the shelf as it was removed by customers. The activity to replace the item by shop employees was triggered by the gap on the shelf created by the customer removing the item.

At home, this pull is obvious when we notice our toothpaste or deodorants are empty. We are triggered to replace them only at that point. Likewise, we generally cook, eat or drink, when we are 'pulled' by our hunger or thirst. Although with food and drink, let's be honest... this isn't always the case! (This simply illustrates an important rule for successful kanban: everyone needs to stick strictly to the rules.)

See for yourself

Try to make your own Kanban board. Use a task list you already have and turn it into a Kanban board. Use three stages: to do, doing, done. What are your 'to do's', what are you 'doing' and what is 'done'. Maybe you have a task list together with a team or with your family. If they are up to an experiment, you can practice a daily scrum with them.

- Do you switch on your central heating when you (or your thermostat) feel cold, or by a timed schedule? The former is pull, the latter is push. Perhaps you need both? This is the same as in many operations (shops, factories, restaurants). Discuss the pros and cons of the alternatives, and when might you select one or other.

Further readings:

Wallace Hopp, *Supply Chain Science*, McGraw Hill, 2008

Ed Pound, Jeffrey Bell, Mark Spearman, *Factory Physics for Managers*, McGraw Hill, 2014

Kevin Duggan, *Creating Mixed Model Value Streams*, Second edition, CRC Press, 2013

Christoph Roser, *All About Pull* Production, All About Lean, 2021

John Bicheno and Matthias Holweg, *The Lean Toolbox: 6th revised edition,* PICSIE books, 2024, Chapter 25

One-piece-flow ideal

The **one-piece-flow ideal** simply means that parts (or products, services, software stages) are made and then moved <u>one at a time</u> instead in batches.

One-piece-flow helps to reduce inventory and improve quality. Quality is improved by getting after any problem quicker and, if there is a defect, not having to scrap or rework the whole batch. Clearly, the one-piece-flow ideal is not always practical – for instance making cookies in an oven. But in this case, the batch is the 'one-piece' instead of making several similar batches one after the other.

Moving to one-piece-flow has huge advantages – most dramatically a cut in lead time. Consider 4 machines with a cycle time of 1 minute per part, each sequentially producing a batch of 10 parts. The batch emerges after 40 minutes. With one-piece-flow, the first part emerges after 4 minutes! The former case is called 'fake flow'. But lead time is only one aspect – dramatic changes in transport (moving away from forklifts?), space, and in early problem detection are also big advantages.

For repetitive work with no changeover, one-piece-flow, instead of moving batches, is much the better way. This is particularly the case where there is a balanced line or cell as in assembly line. Work pieces are moved without interruption along the line.

Sometimes, of course, where parts are small or where a process can only make in batches, one-piece-flow is not feasible. But it is an ideal. Can you move towards the ideal by moving smaller batches or producing smaller batches on a machine (without sacrificing productivity or quality)?

Although cells are widespread, many do not conform to the cell ideal. The ideal cell has one-piece-flow, good visibility, minimal inventories between stations (not zero), and an appropriate organisation. Cell supervisors (team leaders) and Team members identify with the cell as do support functions – quality, maintenance, ideally scheduling.

I am so thirsty

One-piece-flow is closely linked with pull. In a pull system an activity cannot begin without authorisation from an upstream source. Authorisation may be in the form of a kanban card, light, or another signal.

Imagine you're having a few friends round for a drink. Do you make drinks in batches or one at a time? If you make them one at a time it allows the first friend to get their drink quicker than if they must wait for several drinks to be made. They're happy with their thirst quenched. The second drink will arrive shortly after, and so on with others. Ultimately every person in the group will have gotten their drinks earlier in comparison with all having to wait for the full batch to be prepared.

See for yourself

Try the example of making drinks for your friends or family yourself. How much time does it take you to make the drinks in a one-piece-flow and how much time does it take you to do this in a batch. Is there a difference if the drinks are all the same or if everyone chose a different one?

- Or do an experiment: You will need four people. Set up a sequence of four stages. The product is a piece of paper that moves between the stages. You will need a pile of blank papers at the first person. (This represents raw material, orders, enquiries or whatever you wish.) At each stage a person signs their name. The final product therefore has four signatures. Run two experiments of three minutes. In the first, each person signs five papers (products) before passing them on in a batch to the next person. This represents functional or traditional layout. Record the number of completed products. In the second, each person signs only one paper before passing it onto the next person. This represents a cell. Again record the number of completed products. Discuss the results, including the implications for productivity, lead time, and quality.

Further readings:

John Bicheno and Matthias Holweg, *The Lean Toolbox: 6th revised edition,* PICSIE books, 2024

Andon, Poka Yoke and Checklists

An **Andon** is a method (typically a light or a cord) that enables a signal to be given that a problem has been encountered. An Andon is located at a workstation and the operator pulls the cord or switches on a light if a problem occurs.

Poka Yoke is a Japanese term for a device that carries out 100% automatic inspection and either indicates that a problem has occurred or stops work from proceeding.

A **Checklist** is simply a listing of actions, or checks, that are required to be performed prior to a main activity beginning.

This section discusses three widely-use related concepts: Andon, Poka Yoke and Checklists. The three are related because they are all concerned with mistakes or potential mistakes that may result from you or from others.

Andon

A Toyota assembly line is seldom straight – because S shapes are more compact and facilitate communication between sections. Importantly the line is broken into segments with an inventory buffer between segments. This allows the Andon system to work. If a worker experiences a problem, he or she can pull the Andon cord to summon immediate help. If the problem is not resolved within the takt time, the line will stop. The Andon system thus brings worker empowerment to the line – a radical departure from Henry Ford's concept. In addition to the Andon cord, an overhead display board shows production progress, time lost, and problem stations. Music and lights are sometimes used as signalling systems.

The prime role of team leaders is to ensure that their line is running smoothly and producing quality parts. Key to this is their immediate response to Andon alerts. In the second edition of *The Toyota Way* Jeffrey Liker outlines how Team Leaders at Toyota's Burnaston plant in the United Kingdom have 40 core roles defined (Team members have 21). Some of these responsibilities include Andon response, safety, problem solving, team meeting and kaizen. Such is the importance placed on the advanced team leader role that 17 weeks of structured learning are given covering problem solving, leading improvement activities and coaching. The 17 weeks would take several years to complete, on a need, coach, test, verify cycle.

Poka Yoke

The late Shigeo Shingo developed and classified the poka-yoke concept, particularly in manufacturing. Shingo's book *Zero Quality Control: Source Inspection and the Poka Yoke System* is the classic work. More recently C. Martin Hinckley made a significant contribution through his work *Make No Mistake!*

A Poka Yoke (or mistake-proof) device according to Shingo uses '100% automatic inspection together with warning or stop'. Here, key words are 100% and automatic. Note that a poka-yoke is not a control device like a thermostat or toilet control valve that acts every time, but rather a device that senses abnormalities and takes action only when an abnormality is identified. Interestingly, a Poka Yoke can apparently also mean 'distraction–proofing' in Japanese – with implications for using a mobile phone when driving or e-mail interruptions.

Shingo distinguishes between 'mistakes' (which are inevitable) and 'defects' (which result when a mistake reaches a customer). The aim of poka-yoke is to design devices that prevent mistakes becoming defects. According to Shingo there are two categories – those that warn, and those that prevent or control.

There are three types: 'contact', 'fixed value', and 'motion step'. This means that there are six categories. See the table below.

Poka Yoke Types	Control	Warning
Contact	Parking height bars	Shop Entrance Bell
Fixed Value	Pre-dosed medication	Egg tray
Motion Step	Airline lavatory door	Spellcheckers
Adapted from Richard Chase and Douglas Stewart 'Failsafe Service', OMA Conference, 1993		

According to John Grout, areas where Poka Yokes should be considered include areas where worker vigilance is required, where mispositioning is likely, where monitoring is difficult, where external failure costs dramatically exceed internal failure costs, and in mixed model production. Shingo says that Poka Yoke should be thought of as having both a short action cycle (where immediate shut down or warning is given), but also a long action cycle where the reasons for the defect occurring in the first place are investigated. John Grout makes the useful point that one drawback of poka-yoke devices is that potentially valuable information about process variance may be lost, thereby inhibiting improvement.

Hinckley developed an excellent approach to mistake proofing. He developed a classification scheme comprising 10 common categories: omitted operations, omitted parts, wrong orientation, misaligned, wrong location, wrong part, misadjusted, prohibited action, added part, misread instruction. For each category, various mistake proofing solutions have been developed. Thus, having identified the type of mistake, one can look through the set of possible solutions and adapt or select the most suitable one.

There is a continuum of Poka Yokes. Take seatbelts: A weak Poka Yoke would require a driver to use a checklist, including fastening a seatbelt before setting off. A slightly stronger version would require any car passenger to go through the checklist with the driver. A medium strength Poka Yoke would give an audio or display warning when a seatbelt is not fastened. A strong Poka Yoke would prevent the car from starting unless the driver's seatbelt is fastened. The seatbelt example illustrates that the choice of Poka Yoke needs to consider both risk and user acceptance. (Note: This has similarities to the for stages of control in visual management. Forgotten them? Take another look.)

By the way: Andon is not a Poka Yoke. A Poka Yoke requires 100% automatic detection.

Checklists

A checklist is not a true Poka Yoke, but nevertheless is important in reducing mistakes. Of course, a mistake, could be something that is in danger of being forgotten about. A checklist is not automatic, it relies on human conscientiousness, and often requires a change in culture or attitude to be effective. Note that this is not a question of training or competence but a problem of the human brain just having too much to think of, particularly in stressful situations. Surgeons are highly trained but occasionally might leave an instrument inside a patient – due to pressure.

Checklists have received long overdue attention recently due to the work of Atul Gawande's book *The Checklist Manifesto*. Gawande is a Harvard surgeon. The number of errors made in hospitals is truly astounding. From cutting off the wrong limb, to leaving instruments inside a patient, to administering the wrong medicine. Thousands of such cases occur each year in the UK, tens of thousands in USA. Checklists have had remarkable success in reducing such errors, but they require a change in culture – allowing a nurse to go through a checklist for a surgeon (previously a no-no). This is not seen as a reflection of competence, but as a life-saver in a highly stressful, pressurized environment. Gawande points out that checklists have been hundreds of times more cost effective than many new drugs. In fact, new drugs are part of the problem – which one to select? ...and is the most effective drug even known to the doctor?

In the UK, 1 in 16 hospital patients get an infection. This situation has led the deputy head of the health service to encourage patients to carry out their own check: ask the nurse or doctor if they have washed their hands!

It should be noted that a checklist should not be used in high-frequency situations, where a Poka Yoke (mistake-proof) device is far preferable.

Of course, checklists have long been used in aircraft, starting with the B-17 bomber in WW II.

There are the three important points:

1. A checklist must not be too long. (Only the 'key points' in TWI terms.) Perhaps 10 points or less. (A case in point was the crash of an airliner taking off from La Guardia, New York. When the engines failed, the pilot used a checklist but it was too long to complete. Sullenberger nevertheless ditched the aircraft safely in the East River.)
2. A checklist is not a reflection of incompetence, but a recognition that in a focused, stressful situation, important points can be missed. (Have you seen the famous 'Invisible Gorilla' video, where many people counting ball throws simply do not see a man in a gorilla suit walking past!)
3. A checklist of a 'do-confirm' or 'read-do' type is best administered by a second person, again not as a reflection of competence but in recognition that the first person may have many simultaneous things on his or her mind. The second person is therefore helping not hindering. In fact, it has been found that in commercial

aircraft there is a less likelihood of error when the co-pilot is flying rather than the pilot – because the pilot has so many other things to think about.

Given these characteristics, checklists have a great future in service and manufacturing.

May I have your attention, please?

You travel on a bus and wish to get off at the next stop. What do you do? You simply press the button or pull a cord.

How annoying it is to sit in a restaurant, having completed a meal, made conversation, but now wished to depart (you may have booked for a cinema), but cannot attract the waiter's attention for the bill? Well, in India some restaurants have cords hanging down above each table. When you want the waiter, pull the cord. A red light comes on above your table, and within seconds the waiter is there. No problem.

These are both day-to-day examples of an 'Andon' cords. Of course, this is used to attract attention if there is a quality problem, a missing part, or where for some reason there is a delay.

A related issue is to signal to prevent a problem from occurring. This is known as 'Poka Yoke'. 'Poka Yoke' literally means you must prevent (Yoke) inadvertent mistakes (Poka). If you don't like the Japanese term, try 'mistake-proof' or 'fail-safe', but not fool proof – 'fools are so creative!'

There are numerous situations where Poka Yoke is applied. We are sure you have frequently already used a Poka Yoke. Using the earlier table as a guide, suggest another Poka Yoke in each category that you are familiar with.

Yet another related concept is Checklists. Do you make shopping checklists or 'to-do' checklists? We do. They are memory aids but are especially useful when you have so much else to think about.

See For Yourself

Take this week to look around you everywhere you go. Can you spot places where the Andon method is used? Where would you like to add the Andon method? For a variation, think of going to the toilet on a train or a aircraft.....

Same for Poka Yoke: Where can you spot this. It may be in more places than you think. (For hints, see the table earlier in this section.) And where do you see checklists? Or maybe do like to make these yourself?

There are several types of 'pokayoke' (fail safe) device. See the table above. Think of as many as you can of each type. Then check out mistake proofing on the web.

Further readings:

Atul Gawande, *The Checklist Manifesto*, Profile Books, 2011

John Grout's *Mistake-Proofing Centre*, www.mistakeproofing.com

Joseph Hallinan, *Why we make mistakes*, Broadway, 2009

C. Martin Hinckley, *Make No Mistake*, Productivity, 2001

Level Scheduling

A **level schedule** is a smoothed production plan that aims to reduce periods of high activity and periods of low (or no) activity. It is, as far as possible, production at a regular rate.

Many still think that the level schedule is an automotive Lean concept and hence not applicable. This is simply wrong – like the slow cooker story in the Postponement section. The level schedule can almost always be applied to a good proportion of products. Here we consider the 'why' for a schedule to be as level as possible.

Why is a level schedule such a worthwhile aim, and such a potent driving force:

- Muri and Mura are often cited as the root causes of Muda. Mura (unevenness) is directly related to level scheduling. Muri (overburden) causes instability and leads to instable schedules. With unevenness, as utilization increases towards 100% of capacity, delays build exponentially and the uncertainty of schedule attainment increases.
- Fast problem identification is facilitated by level schedules. Visual management is made easier. As soon as a schedule deviates from plan it is noticed, and the root cause sought.
- The level schedule facilitates Lean or cell layout, the small machine concept, and value streams.
- Everyone works better with no surprises.
- And how about level schedules for management? This is the essence of what David Mann says about Lean Leadership – standard work for managers with meetings held at standard, regular times. In short, predictable level schedules.
- Internally, delivery schedules are smoothed. A tugger (or runner) can be set up. Material handling is much more efficient. Perhaps a plant can stop using forklift trucks for big batches.
- In Design, Intel and others level their Design process, bringing out new generations of chips on a regular cycle.
- Level scheduling extends to suppliers and to customers – end to end along the supply chain. Suppliers appreciate regular orders and delivery schedules – this enables them to become Lean themselves. Likewise, if customers place regular orders, flow is made much easier, and inventory is reduced.

Complete levelling of operations may not be possible. However, there are many actions that can be taken to facilitate levelling. One is Demand Analysis, discussed under the Planning and Organising Fishbone, and others are Changeover Reduction, and the Base Schedule discussed under the Preparing Fishbone.

Closely related to Level Scheduling is Mixed Model Scheduling. Mixed Model Scheduling means scheduling Part A, Part B, and Part C in the manner: **ABC, ABC, ABC**.... in a repeating sequence rather than in three separate large batches of A, B, and C. There are several reasons for this: it is a powerful aid to cell and line balancing (by placing long cycle items next to short cycle items), it reduces work-in-process (WIP) inventory and sometimes finished goods inventory, it may lead to better customer service, and (a big one) it results in a constant rate of flow of parts to the line or cell by material handling, rather than at different rates for different products. Mixed Model Scheduling may also mean more interesting work for operators.

In assembly operations with no changeover, mixed model operations are most desirable. It is particularly advantageous when products with different assembly times come down a line, such as in a car plant. Here a 'complex' car is followed by a 'simple' car. This is much better for flow and material handing than having all 'complex' cars followed by all 'simple' cars, which would imply different rates of working. In automotive, mixed model lines now send both cars and vans down the same line.

Level Scheduling and Mixed Model Scheduling are facilitated by a Heijunka box or system whereby a day's production or activity is split into equal time slots. This is also called 'day-by-the-hour' scheduling. These are also a quality and improvement tool. If production during a time slot is missed, this is known immediately, and the reason is sought.

	7:00-8:00	8:00-9:00	9:00-10:00	10:00-11:00
Product A	A	A	A	A
Product B	B		B	
Product C		C		C
Product D	D	D	D	D
Product E	E	E	E	E

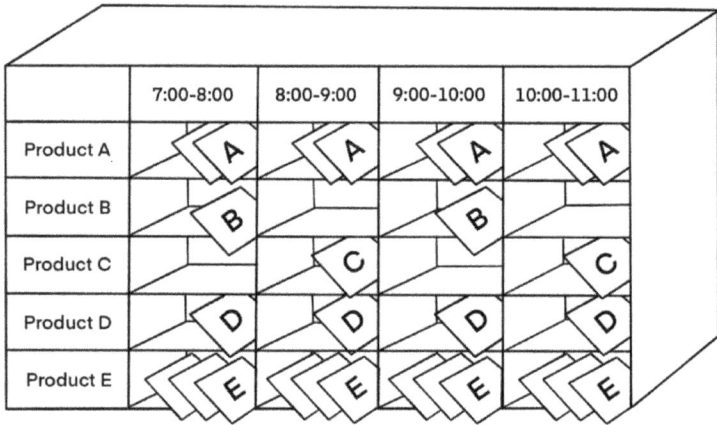

Stay in balance

We all have a series of tasks required of us each day. They can be work life or home life related. What needs to be done (Planning) and when they need to be done (scheduling) can be balanced in a mixed model fashion to ease the burden of the physical or mental (cognitive) load.

When cooking, you often use a form of mixed model scheduling. Perhaps you are cooking risotto, mushrooms, and carrots. You stir the risotto, stir the mushrooms, then cut the carrots. This is done over a number of cycles. Probably if you did the cooking in three separate batches it would take longer and not taste as good.....

Some physically demanding or laborious tasks can be scheduled and mixed throughout your day or week with less physical but more mentally demanding tasks. (This is the equivalent of switching from one product type to another.) This allows for more balanced use of both types of capacity throughout your day or week.

This is of course massively assisted by making sure only the required tasks are planned (pull) and the switch from one task or activity to another is efficient and effective (Changeover reduction).

This mixed model approach to planning and scheduling your day or week can lead to a sustainable use of your physical and mental capacity, whilst ensuring all tasks required get completed in a steady progressive manner. One of the additional benefits to this is that your day or week has variety and more stimulation than just large bodies of repetitive tasks done in bulk.

See For Yourself

Think about your key daily or weekly activities, work/school and free time:

- Can you plan your activities in such a way that each day is as busy as the other days?
- What is a good mix of your activities in a day? (Perhaps, if you are writing a long report, you could have breaks for tea or coffee. Give your brain a break?)
- What would you do differently if you would implement this?
- How could you schedule them in a mixed model approach?

Further readings:

John Bicheno and Matthias Holweg, *The Lean Toolbox: 6th revised edition,* PICSIE books, 2024

Kanban Board

A **Kanban board** is a visual tool to manage and visualize the flow of work within a team. It is particularly associated with the Kanban methodology.

In Agile software development, a level schedule is facilitated by a Kanban Board. The Kanban board provides a clear and transparent way to visualize work items, their status, and the workflow. Here's how it works:

1. Columns and Cards:
    Columns: The board is divided into columns representing different stages of the workflow. Common columns include "To Do," "In Progress," "Testing," and "Done."
    Cards: Work items, often represented by cards, move through these columns from left to right as they progress through the development process.

2. Work in Progress (WIP) Limits:
    Each column might have a Work in Progress (WIP) limit, indicating the maximum number of items allowed in that column simultaneously. WIP limits help prevent overloading the team from and encourage a smoother flow of work. (Remember 'Muri'?)

3. Visualization:
    The Kanban board provides a visual representation of the current status of each work item. Team members and stakeholders can quickly see what tasks are in progress, what is completed, and what is in the backlog.

4. Continuous Flow:
    Kanban emphasizes a continuous flow of work. As soon as a task is completed in one column, the team can pull in the next item from the backlog, ensuring a steady and efficient workflow.

5. Prioritisation:
    Work items are often prioritized on the Kanban board, with the most important tasks placed at the top. This allows the team to focus on delivering the highest-priority features first.

6. Adaptability:
    Kanban is inherently adaptable. It allows teams to respond to changes quickly. If priorities shift or new tasks

emerge, they can be added to the backlog and reprioritized as needed.

7. Collaboration:
   The Kanban board promotes collaboration among team members. Everyone can see the status of each task, which fosters communication and coordination.

8. Metrics and Continuous Improvement:
   Teams using Kanban often track metrics such as cycle time (how long it takes to complete a task) and lead time (how long it takes from request to completion). These metrics help identify areas for improvement and optimize the development process continually.

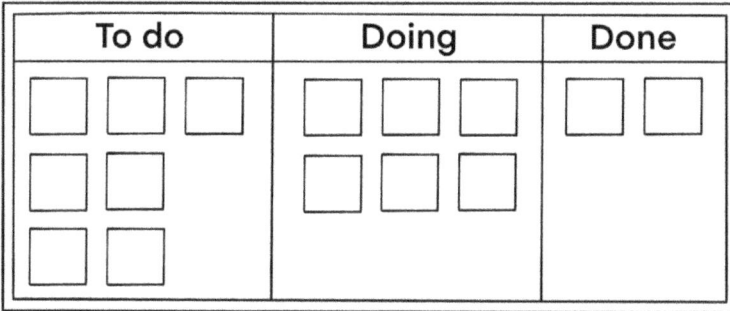

To do	Doing	Done

A Kanban board in Agile software development is a visual representation of the team's work, providing transparency, promoting collaboration, and facilitating the continuous flow of tasks through the development process.

What to do?

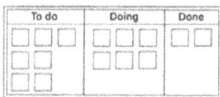

Staying on top of a busy household is no easy feat. Think of all the activities involved in your average family home. Who needs to do what when? Who needs picking up at what time?

Whose responsibility is it do order something, call someone, or walk the dog? How do we know when these are planned or when they have been done?

Quite often the best solutions are the simplest. A kanban board on the fridge with magnets that you can move to different compartments is a very useful solution. For example, a magnet that clarifies who should walk the dog. And when you have done it, move the magnet to the 'Done' section of the board. Simple, but effective.

See for yourself

Try to make your own Kanban board. Use a task list you already have and turn it into a Kanban board. Or, if you don't have one use planning your next holiday. Use three stages: to do, doing, done. What are your 'to do's', what are you 'doing' and what is 'done'. Maybe you have a task list together with a team or with your family. If they are up to an experiment, you can practice a daily scrum with them.

But maybe you can find more places where this can be useful? At your sports club? Or.....?

Further readings:

Charles Duhigg, *The Power of Habit*, Heinemann, 2012

James Clear, *Atomic Habits*, RH Books, 2018

Robert Maurer, *One Small Step Can Change Your Life: The Kaizen Way*, Workman, 2004

Atul Gawande, *The Checklist Manifesto*, Profile Books, 2011

John Grout's *Mistake-Proofing Centre*,
www.mistakeproofing.com

Joseph Hallinan, *Why we make mistakes*, Broadway, 2009

C. Martin Hinckley, *Make No Mistake*, Productivity, 2001

John Bicheno and Matthias Holweg, *The Lean Toolbox: 6th revised edition*, PICSIE books, 2024, Chapters 14, 25, 26, 40

Christoph Roser, *All About Pull Production*, All About Lean, 2021

Amy Edmondson, *The Fearless Organisation*, Wiley, 2019

Gwendolyn Galsworth, *Work that makes sense*, Visual Lean, 2011

David Sibbet, *Visual Meetings*, Wiley, 2010

Richard Moore and Lisa Schienkopf, *Theory of Constraints and Lean Manufacturing Friends or Foes?* Chesapeake Consulting Inc., 1998 (Supplied by Goldratt Institute)

Wallace Hopp, *Supply Chain Science*, McGraw Hill, 2008

Ed Pound, Jeffrey Bell, Mark Spearman, *Factory Physics for Managers*, McGraw Hill, 2014

Kevin Duggan, *Creating Mixed Model Value Streams*, Second edition, CRC Press, 2013

Improving

How to do better?

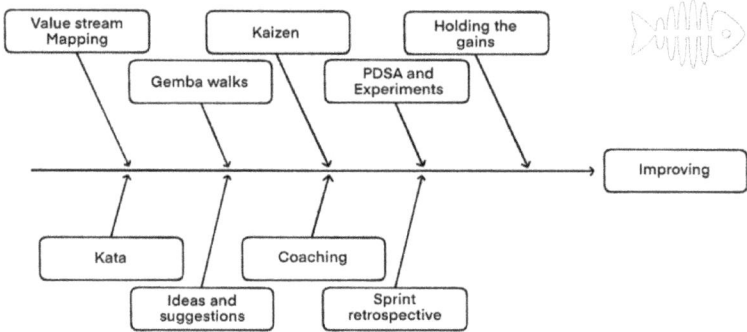

On your bike again…

To make it to the very end of the journey isn't about just blindly spinning the wheels. Even though the journey is challenging, we don't want to just survive; we want to thrive. This will require an almost habitual mindset to be curious, to discover, to discuss, to respond, and to improve.

- Does everyone on our journey know what behaviours are essential to improving?
- Do we really understand how everyone is managing with their part in the journey?
- Do we need to be more specific in our understanding of our performance, or what we're trying to do?
- How can we keep this pace, but aim to go faster without fatigue or crashing?
- How do we make some changes, try something new, and listen to the experience of the team members?

All of these questions are essential to Lean and Agile and the philosophy of continuous improvement. To answer them is a collective effort and based on a platform of wanting to improve, and respecting each other's thoughts, feelings, and contributions.

Value Stream Mapping

Value Stream Mapping is a method of documenting, quantifying, and analysing the series of steps from an agreed start point to an agreed end point.

The purpose is to identify wastes and opportunities for improvement to provide greater customer value. An important feature is that is traces the horizontal flow of products or services, often from supplier all the way through to the customer.

Value Stream Mapping is a three-stage process, and in Rother and Shook's 'Learning to See' the Current State, Future State and Action Plans is presented as a trilogy in mapping and transformation:

1. *Current State:* The need for change must be recognised. The 'why'. This involves recording current performance and identifying gaps. Then the need to change must be communicated. Not just communicated but explained and discussed in detail.
2. *Future State:* The next stage, where we are going, must be worked out and explained. The vision. Based on the current performance gaps, what changes can be made to

the process to create an improved process? What would a newer, reduced waste, and much improved process look like? This new 'future state' is exactly that. It gives direction and focus to our improvement activities.

3. ***Action Plan:*** The plan to get there must be agreed. The 'What' (planning) and the 'when' (scheduling) and agreements of 'who' is responsible for the action taken, ideally with an agreed deadline. Quite often these action plans take the form of a project sequence chart and are used to drive the implementation of the Future state.

A general summary of drawing a Value Stream Map is described below. This must be done at the Gemba with the team:

1. ***Walk the map.*** In other words, 'go to the Gemba' and directly observe. Do not attempt to draw a Current State Map by sitting in an office and trying to remember. A great value is walking the value stream from end to end. (See "Gemba walks' section below.)

2. ***Link the steps.*** Visually link the steps within the process with arrows that show either 'push' or 'pull' activities.

3. ***Add a data box.*** On the map, place a 'data box' below each step. This will be where all critical data relevant to that particular step will be recorded and made visible.

4. ***Gather the data in the data box.*** Data is key to a deeper understanding of the process and its performance. This data normally includes:
   - **Process time and Changeover time:** record the process time of each step as well as any changeover time (if required)
   - **Batch size:** include the batch size and make notes if batch sizes vary. Also include the number operators. Use full time equivalents (FTE's).
   - **Rejects and Rework amounts:** include notes on the occurrence at each step. For rework, indicate the rework loop. Show the locations and quantities of any safety stocks.

- **Variation:** especially at shared and critical resources. For most purposes simply estimate process variation time as low, medium, or high.
- **Reliability (failure rate):** make notes regarding tracked reliability of the process, ideally mean time between failures (MTBF), and mean time to repair (MTTR).
- **Inventory quantity and storage types:** add the current inventory that is found between the process steps. Show this below an inventory triangle symbol. Draw in the means of physical replenishment of inventory, such as a kanban loop or 'runner' frequency. The storage types can be defined as follows:
  - *Supermarkets*: simply a store where components are kept.
  - *Buffer stocks*: part-completed products held between stages or finished products waiting to be moved onwards. Show the locations and quantities.
- **Takt time:** Available time / Average Demand. Note: For a 'shared resource' (being a machine that is used by more than one value stream), takt time may not be useful, but for downstream operations it can be a powerful concept that sets the overall drumbeat rate.

5. **Analyse each step for wastes** (either Manufacturing or Service). Use the awareness and understanding of the wastes (Muda, Mura, Muri) to analyse each step. If required, discuss with team members to decide whether each activity is a waste and has the potential to be removed because it is unnecessary and not Value Adding. Be aware that some steps, whilst not Value Adding, are Necessary Non-Value Adding and must remain due to regulatory or safety requirements.

6. **Identify opportunities for improvement**, also known as 'Kaizen Bursts'. Beyond identifying wastes, many team members may be triggered to highlight potentials for improvement at various parts of the map based on

wastes and issues discovered. These can be 'captured' and simply added to the map as a 'kaizen burst', a little icon or idea bubble for what can potentially be changed at this point in the future state process.

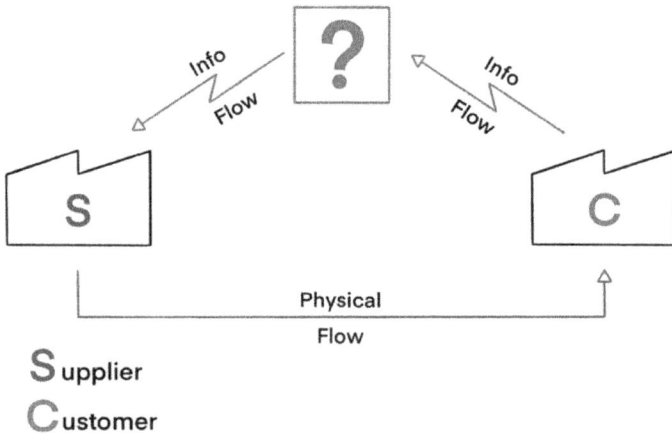

S upplier

C ustomer

Note: This example of a Future State Map, shown above, shows the long-term aspirations. Most Future State maps would show an intermediate state. In the example, a cell is shown at the centre, followed by a supermarket symbol. A Heijunka box draws products from the supermarket to go to shipping. As products are withdrawn from the supermarket, a kanban card pulls parts from the pre-cell supermarket to go into the cell. And as parts are withdrawn from the pre-cell supermarket, parts are pulled from the post-press supermarket. Pulling these parts from the post-press supermarket results in cards accumulating in a batch box. When sufficient cards of a particular part have accumulated in the batch box to justify a batch being made, the kanban authority to make the batch goes into the pre-press queue. Raw material is pulled into the press from the pre-press supermarket.

To create the future state and ideal state diagrams requires two steps:

1. First, visually incorporate the previously mentioned short-term improvements in to the new Future State

map. This means, redrawing the process but without the waste and non-value adding steps where possible. This will now look like a 'new' process and should ideally show consideration to the 'kaizen bursts' from the team members so that improved ways of working are now part of the 'future state' process map.

2. The second step requires more in-depth knowledge of Lean possibilities. These are the subjects of the Planning and Preparing fishbones discussed in earlier Chapters. It is often useful to break up the value steam map into 'pull segments' or 'loops', often separated by buffers of inventory. This will enable you to begin to eliminate, combine, rearrange, simplify. (The four classic improvement actions.)

A very useful, and fun, aid in developing the future state map is Simon Dodds' 4N Chart as shown below (Used with permission).

The team starts at the bottom-left and focuses on current negative feelings. These are the Niggles. Apply 5 Why to these Niggles. Then focus on the positive feelings that are generated by the current situation. These Nuggets are features that should be retained. Then come the No Nos that the team would certainly like to be rid of. Finally, the Nice Ifs are features that the team would like more of – aspects that generate positive feelings, like visual indicators.

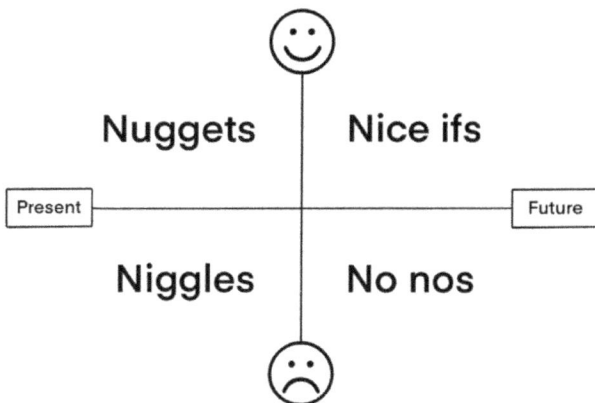

Note that the Learning to See map discussed above is but one of 7 basic map types. The family of maps comprise Brown paper, 'Learning to See', Information flow, Spaghetti, Quality filter, Demand amplification, Financial map. Details of these other maps are given in The Lean Toolbox.

A good map needs eyes and ears...

Most people are familiar with maps and use them regularly. They are especially helpful in getting you get from A to B. When we use, for example Google Maps, it not only tells us what is located between point A and point B, but also tells us how long it will take to get there, and specifically where the delays and bottlenecks are (highlighted in red or amber). This helps to suggest an alternative route.

Even better is to look at the map together with people who regularly use the route so they can provide advice and suggestions. They know the pitfalls to avoid, traffic cameras and good places to stop. Perhaps they suggest a different means of transport to get to your destination. Of course, delays and bottlenecks are a waste of your time, and traffic cameras can cost you money.

This procedure you could think of as the current state basic map. A more insightful, more advisable map, with actions to take and to avoid.

See for yourself

Can you make a value stream map? What process would like to improve? Maybe the process of getting up in the morning and going to work/school.

- Go to the Gemba, look and listen, collect data and draw a VSM for the current state.
- Look for bottlenecks, flow problems, quality issues, and excessive inventory.

- Add the 4N chart.
- Draw out a preliminary future state map.
- What action plan do you have if you see the difference between current and future state?
- Doing this is even more fun if you do this with a team. Everyone must be involved in the process to have a good contribution.

Further readings:

Mike Rother and John Shook, *Learning to See*, The Lean Enterprise Institute, Brookline, MA, 1998. The classic reference

Karen Martin and Mike Osterling, *Value Steam Mapping*, McGraw Hill, 2014. A useful reference particularly on organising the mapping team

Mark Nash and Sheila Poling, *Mapping the Total Value Stream*, CRC Press, 2008. A useful reference particularly on mapping mechanics.

John Bicheno and Matthias Holweg, *The Lean Toolbox*, Revised 6th revised edition, PICSIE Books, 2024

Gemba walks

A **Gemba walk** is a walk taken by managers along a value stream, often end-to-end, during which time they observe, ask, and learn first-hand of its status, good or bad.

Gemba means 'actual place' and is used to refer to the place where work is being carried out.

Gemba Walks are now widely found not just in factories, but in many service operations also. Gemba walks are sometimes known as 'waste walks'. A walk involves the action of leaders going to see the actual processes, understanding the work, asking probing questions, and learning from those who do the work. By so doing, leaders not only learn the issues first hand but demonstrate humility and that people are the critical value adders. The objective is to understand the value stream and its problems, rather than to review results or make superficial comments from their office or conference room.

(In English, some people talk about 'at the coalface'. If you don't like the Japanese 'Gemba' word, would you prefer 'Coalface'?)

The purpose of a Gemba Walk is sometimes not understood, so the potential is lost, and it may do more harm than good. So, what are the characteristics of a good Gemba Walk?

- Purpose: teaching and supporting others and learning about the processes and people.
- Focus: on the work not blaming the person or issuing instructions.
- Time: allowing sufficient time for discussion and for follow up.
- Assignments: agree on what to do.
- Follow up: from issues arising on the previous walk.
- Objective: asking with curiosity. Seeking mutual understanding of issues. 'Can you show me…',
- Servant Leadership: Identifying obstacles that need to be removed by management so that flow can be improved.
- Communication and Trust: Building working relationships
- Emphasise the value stream, not vertical silos
- Follow up with line managers as to the agreed next steps.

In summary, good Gemba practice is acronym ALLL: **Ask, Look, Listen, Learn**

Remember them ALLL!

What a Gemba Walk is NOT is:

- A casual, or rapid, walk-through or tour.

- Management merely showing their face or flag waving on the shop floor or office.
- An inspection – demanding action on anything out of place that is spotted, or to catch people out.
- A routine walk-through, following the same route.
- Giving answers. Telling.
- Giving direct orders on the spot, rather than coaching front line leaders.

A summary of Gemba Walks is the 7 G's:

1. **GO** to the actual place.
2. **GET** the facts from the actual situation by direct observation.
3. **GATHER** ideas and suggestions. Ask and listen – very little tell, unless asked.
4. **GIVE** credit where due.
5. **GRASP** the current condition and clarify any problem.
6. **GUIDE** the implementation through support, coaching, and feedback.
7. **GENERATE** and agree improvement proposals together with the people at the gemba. (Establish the next target situation. This will often mean breaking down the problem into manageable chunks.)

In an office or factory, a Gemba Walk would involve following the value stream, not just going to a particular point.

A good Gemba Walk means that team leaders and workers get an opportunity to be heard, and to demonstrate pride in their work and achievements. Leaders, at all levels, learn respect, have the opportunity to coach, and better to understand people and process.

See the earlier section on Listening and Questioning. This will make a Gemba Walk much more effective.

Finally, from Michael Marquardt in *Leading with Questions:*

"I thought a managers' job was to provide answers, to provide solutions…. But I came to realize how disempowering this is, and

how much more effective I could be by posing the question back to the person with the problem... It is much more effective to provide the opportunity for them to solve their own problems."

Visible curiosity

Gemba walks affect everyone involved, the leader doing the walk, and those in the area being 'walked'. Think about your household. Maybe you're a busy parent out working, and managing day to day tasks within the house, not just the bills, but the appointments and the activities the children are involved in. It's difficult to stay involved in what is happening in every room, with everybody, every day.

Perhaps you are still living at home and are seeing from a distance the different roles you all play in your household.

Going to Gemba would involve the parents who are essential for leading the family and running the household successfully, actively engaging and enquiring as to the current situation family members in the house are in. Actually going to the person's room or study area, asking 'how are things going?' shows more interest than asking the same question at breakfast. Maybe there is some help required? Maybe there is an issue that needs to be resolved? Maybe a suggestion to bring everyone closer or improve how we all live together? "What support do you need from me?".

The power of this 'visible curiosity' in the area of the people that matter most, brings you closer to the potential issues and suggestions - it shows that you care and are interested. It is also a chance to demonstrate that you are open for feedback, and that they have a voice and will be heard.

See for yourself

Try a Gemba walk at your sports club, or gym, or local shop. Don't call it a Gemba walk or announce that you are doing one. Just say, for instance, 'I have been looking around in the____and have noticed _____'. Use the first 5 of the 7 'G's'.

- How do you see things differently if you look at this through Gemba-walk glasses
- What questions would you ask the people around you?

Further readings:

Masaaki Imai, *Gemba Kaizen*, McGraw-Hill, New York, 1997

Jim Womack, *Gemba Walks, Second edition*, Lean Enterprise Institute

---

Kaizen

Kaizen is a Japanese word meaning 'good change' and 'improvement for the better'. Although Kaizen can apply to both big and small changes, often it is the many small changes that are the dominant focus. Kaizen involves participation by all, but especially by front-line people.

Maasaki Imai wrote the classic text 'Kaizen' in 1986. Imai describes how kaizen can be applied to Muda, Muri, and Mura each under headings of people, techniques, methods, time, facilities and more. Imai also set out how kaizen applies to each of the 5S steps, and to problem solving involving: who, what, where, when, why, and how, as well as the well-known sequence 'eliminate, combine, rearrange, simplify'. The use of the PDSA cycle is a basic requirement of Kaizen.

Kaizen influences many (or perhaps all) of all the elements in all the Fishbones in this publication.

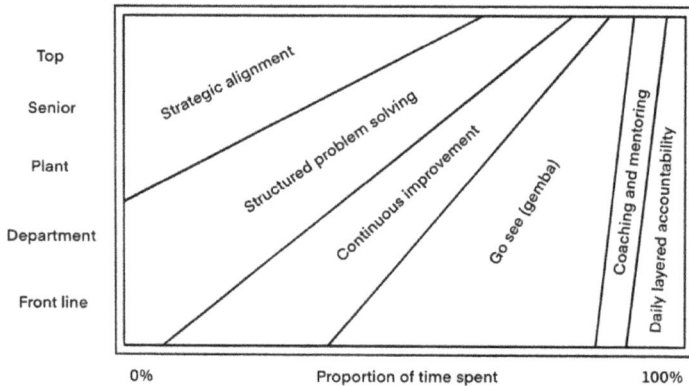

An important idea is Imai's 'Kaizen Flag'. The version above is adapted from Imai's original. It shows organisation level along the vertical axis and proportion of time spent along the horizontal axis. Generally, as one moves vertically so the emphasis changes from taking waste out, to keeping waste out to designing and creating strategic value.

The more you look, the more you find...

Our day is filled with countless opportunities for improvement. From slight irritations, to small performance issues. A delay here, a miscommunication there. We see typos in documents, we have doors that stick, and shelves too crammed. We have documents we always struggle to find, or a leaking tap we need to fix.

Improvement doesn't have to be sweeping and dramatic, quite often too much and too soon can be a recipe for disaster. Small, frequent, incremental steps across the board and in the right direction tend have a huge impact over time. They also tend to stay embedded.

The truth is, the more we look, the more we find. Finetuning our eyes to 'things not perfect' presents us with hundreds of opportunities for 'kaizen' and the benefits that come with it.

As this finetuning becomes routine, so does a habitual mindset for improvement.

Kaizen events

Kaizen events fill the gap between individual, local improvement initiatives and bigger initiatives such as value steam improvement. They are a means to get cross-functional and multi-level teams involved in a Lean transformation. In that respect, kaizen events have a dual role – they make improvements but also teach and communicate. An important and stimulating aspect of kaizen events is that they are done over a very short period of time, thereby allowing manager involvement that might otherwise not be possible. Often, the results of a Kaizen Event are dramatic, but a common problem is actually sustaining the improvements made.

What comes to mind when one says 'Kaizen Event' is the 5-day variety. However, 'Mini Kaizens' taking from half a day to two days are a useful variant, and have become more popular.

What is described below is the full 5-day variety.

A kaizen event requires pre-event preparation, and possibly training. An event typically involves a team of about 7 people, comprising managers, workers, and a Lean facilitator. All must devote 5 days full-time. The following schedule is typical for a 5-day event:

- **Day 1:** Introductions, aims and scope, background – why is the event important, event methodology, basic Lean training including mapping, waste awareness, tools such as fishbone diagram, and if relevant, practice on observation timing.
- **Day 2:** Go to the area and observe, map the routings, time durations, discuss the process with the people. Possibly the customers in some types of services. Many offices have longer cycle operations so it may not be possible to observe or time all activities, so tagging or simulation may be used. If possible, observe several cycles. Begin to generate ideas.
- **Day 3:** Idea generation, discussion around the maps and formulate priorities and the implementation plan.

Discuss with office workers and other shifts. Begin implementation.

- **Day 4:** The main day for implementation. Try out and adjust. Begin to prepare flipcharts for the presentation on Day 5. Measure results.
- **Day 5:** A final check and adjust. Document the new process. List follow up items. Prepare an A3 summary sheet. Finish flipcharts for presentation. Present to area managers and directors. Agree next steps. Enjoy the free buffet.

After the event it is necessary to:

- Close off any outstanding points. The persons responsible for doing these mopping-up mini-projects must be identified. The event champion or a line manager MUST follow these up. Kaizen events lose credibility if the list of outstanding topics are never closed down.
- Have a review session every (say) month for a period of (say) 6 months. These may be very short meetings. But they look at the continuing performance of the area and, importantly, record lessons learned.

PDSA and Experiments

The essence of science is experiments: Think of a new way. Try it out and study to see if it works. Either way, you learn: you know it does not work, or it seems to work and further development is possible.

PDSA

PDSA (Plan, Do, Study, Adjust) also known as the Deming Cycle has become the standard improvement and learning method in the Lean world.

Synonymous with the experimental method, it should be used for problem solving to test plans and hypotheses. Often PDSA is shown as a cycle, but it actually alternates between theory (plan and adjust) and implementation (do and study):

- **Planning** is about formulating a proposal, plan or hypothesis
- **Do** is about carrying out the plan
- **Study** is about comparing the outcome with the hypothesis, and then learning any lessons
- **Adjust** is tweaking and re-standardising, ready for the next cycle.

Two points about PDSA:

1. It requires time to go through the cycle
2. It is more suitable for recurring processes

Scientific method assumes a repeatable experiment. If there is a chaotic or complex situation this may not be the case.

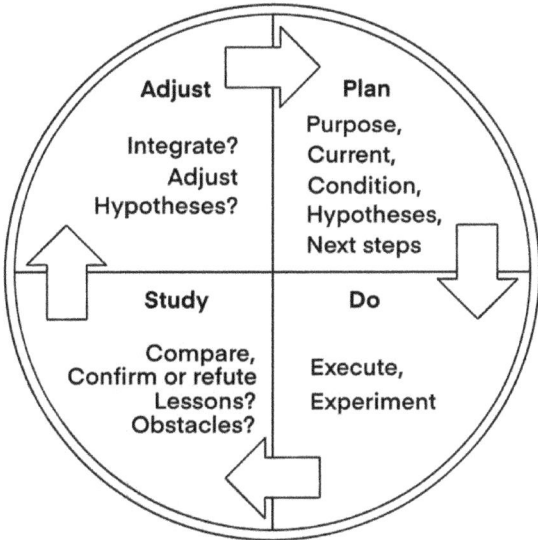

Too often, improvement is seen as one-off, uni-directional, having no clear prediction, no comparison with prediction, and no learning potential. It is PD not PDSA. If this is the case it may be a project but is not scientific method. This brings us to Experiments.

Experiments

An **experiment** is a scientific procedure to test hypotheses or investigate phenomena. It involves manipulating variables while keeping others constant, observing and measuring effects.

The 'gold standard' today for an experiment is the randomised trial, or A/B test. Or even better the (blind) randomised trial. A pure randomised trial involves a randomly selected experimental group and a control group. This is much better than the widespread use of correlation studies that are subject to a large number of unknown external factors. Randomised trials are the standard in healthcare but remain underused in operations. Why? Often not easy to do, but there are opportunities where, for example, there are parallel assembly lines or dozens of people working in a service centre. Of course, a full scientific approach would today (especially in healthcare) require a randomised trial.

A/B experiments have grown strongly. The 'A' is the current approach or method, and the 'B' is the challenger. A/B tests are ideal for on-line web site improvements, but the method can also be used in many service and logistics environments. It is now widely used by, amongst others, Amazon, Google, Sky, Microsoft who conduct hundreds of experiments each month. A widely used approach is used for web-site layout where small changes in the web site design are evaluated by thousands of users, without the users being aware that a test is being conducted. The thousands of users allow for good statistical validity. An A/B test is often superior to a focus group but is not always possible. (Focus groups suffer from the possibility of Groupthink, Confirmation bias, member selection, and Psychological Safety. See the Problem Solving Chapter and the Motivating and Measuring Chapter).

Although very seldom possible in operations rather than research, do think about the possibility – for instance, with two cells, making a change in one cell but not in the other and observing the difference.

In Lean an experiment is very often a small step. Small steps are also the essence of 'The Lean Startup' methodology. Here, instead of spending huge amounts of time on lengthy project definition, design and specification, an experimental approach is used which tests out a 'minimal viable product'. (MVP). Here a basic or cut-down version of a product or service is tested in an A/B experiment. Where the test succeeds the product is gone ahead with; where it fails it is abandoned. It's a low risk and learning methodology. Fail fast and learn.

Finally in this section….

Teruyuki Minoura, MD of Global Purchasing at Toyota says *"When production stops everyone is forced to solve the problem immediately. So team members have to think and, through thinking, team members grow and become better team members and people."* TPS, he says, is *"a manufacturing process where he or she alone must decide what needs to be made and how quickly it needs to be made… It's a basic characteristic of human beings that they develop wisdom from being put under pressure."* …and *"There can be no successful monozukuri (making thing) without hito-zukuri (making people). To keep coming up with revolutionary new production techniques, we need to develop unique ideas and knowledge by thinking about problems in terms of genchi genbutsu. This means it's necessary to think about how we can develop people who can come up with these ideas."* (From media.toyota.co.uk, 2003)

What we get from this is

- Problems must be brought to the surface and be made clearly visible
- Some decisions must be made quickly and at the front line
- Problems are opportunities for improvement, not just restoration
- Problems are a route to developing people

Many of the tools discussed in earlier sections can be regarded as problem-surfacing tools. For example kanban, andon, and poka yoke can give rapid indications of things not proceeding as they should. A first step is to ask why it did not proceed as it should. This is then an opportunity for an experiment. But an over-riding requirement is a no-fears climate – a climate where problems are seen as opportunities.

We'll never know unless we try

We all make changes almost every day. Most of these changes are small things – perhaps changing a cooking cycle time, running or swimming a small extra distance, leaving your bike locked up in another location, trying a different route to work. But the crucial question is, do we learn from making the change? Trying things for the first time can sometimes yield valid conclusions, but often, due to variations in the way we did it or the environment we did it in, the effect of the change is not apparent or leads to a wrong conclusion.

We want to try new things and get better, but it is important to know what we did, how we did it, and in what environment, to make sure we understand fully how we got the results we did. Understanding the process we are using for experimenting is critical, not just the result of the experiment.

See for yourself

What would you like to change in your life? This should be a small thing – for example try out the layout of furniture in your room, changing one ingredient in a recipe, or a new exercise at your gym. Now think like a scientist. Choose the subject and try the steps:

- What is your new **Plan?** (Or layout, or recipe, or exercise.)
- Let's **Do** this!
- How did it go? **Study** it. What are your lessons or conclusions?

- **Adjust** the plan and take the next step in improving your life.

Alternatively, perhaps a recipe did not work out as expected, or you arrived late for a lecture or cinema. Ask why. Then try a PDSA experiment next time.

Remember, it is sometimes said that insanity is doing the same thing over and over again, but expecting a different result. This is the opposite of PDSA!

Further readings:

John Bicheno, *The Service Systems Toolbox*, PICSIE, 2012

Stefan Thomke, *Experimentation Works*, Harvard Business Review Press, 2020

Holding the gains

Holding the gains means not slipping back to a previous less satisfactory way of doing things.

The first point to make is that, like perpetual motion, there is no such thing as 'self-sustainability'. The Second Law of Thermodynamics, (or Entropy) sometimes called the supreme law of the universe, says that unless you put energy into a system it will run down, degrade into disorder and, eventually, death (as in no energy). The natural state is chaos! The same applies to Lean project sustainability. But there are greater risks; without the right sort of energy the system will degrade very rapidly.

The amazing story of Wiremold is a case in point. After 12 years of hugely successful Lean transformation, the company had become one of the Lean showpieces in North America. It was written up in the book *Lean Thinking*. Yet three years after being taken over, many of the measures of performance had declined to what Bob Emiliani (who wrote a case study on the success of the company) describes as 'batch and queue'.

There are many failure modes that result in not holding the gains. For example:

- Diminishing senior management support and respect. This typically wanes sometime after the initial improvements. Leader standard work (LSW) is a good solution. (See Solving Problems Chapter.) And the related practice of senior managers not visiting front line customer support locations.
- Lack of 'Bottom Line' impact. Many Lean initiatives impact quality, delivery, and morale but take time to feed though to financial impact. Some managers then lose patience and say 'Lean has failed'.
- Competing initiatives. Lean, Six Sigma, Agile, OpEx, AI, IT systems, automation all distract. For example, some of the original companies that championed Six Sigma have begun to back down. GE is a classic example. Others, like 3M (according to Klein) have found that Six Sigma has inhibited innovation. Yet others have trained too many black belts. (Some is good, so more must be better!). They have then found that there are insufficient high-level projects.
- Lean is seen as a short-term fix. It is not. Certainly, if Lean is seen as "Less Employees Are Needed" or headcount reduction, then it will fail.

Losing weight without yoyoing

We've all tried to save money and we've all tried to lose weight. Quite often we make some big gains early through extra focus and motivation. But what about after that initial burst of energy and motivation starts to drop? What about the other areas of focus such as work deadlines or other objectives that start to take a share of your energy and focus? What about when the people in

149

your life start to be affected by this new lifestyle or diet? It's not easy saying no to a reward or a treat after a demanding week.

A new lifestyle will take time to become normal. It takes time to adjust to not eating the things you used to eat, or not spending money on previous items or activities. When doing anything new, especially with regards to behaviours, there will be bumps in the road and struggles. To 'hold the gains' is to maintain your recent weight loss, before aiming at your new target. It means managing your lifestyle on the new budget. This leads to consistent savings. It means the recent benefits and improvements can be maintained (weight lost and money saved), and that the 'new' behaviours are no longer new, but have become the regular way (or habits) you live day to day, and week to week.

Unlike a degree, some professional qualifications require periodic re-testing to make sure that the recipient has remained up-to-date. Beware of some Lean 'qualifications' that do not require re-testing!

See for yourself

Have you tried the 'Plan, Do, Study, Adjust' from last Chapter? Let's try to maintain your progress.

- Can you come up with three ideas for you so you can hold your gains?
- And do you know when it is really hard to keep up your good work? Where can you put your positive energy?
- Put temptation away from risk. Move those chocolates out of sight, move other items into sight so they get noticed. Set reminders for good new practices until they become established as habits.

Kata

Kata is a routine or sequence of actions that are learned by repetition and coaching such that they become a habit or automatic reaction.

Maybe you heard connected with martial arts, like Karate, Similarly, in Lean and Agile, a Kata is a routine that helps to develop a scientific approach to improvement.

Kata (or 'Toyota Kata' as it known – after books on the topic by author Mike Rother) is sometimes mistaken as a problem- solving methodology. But in fact, Toyota Kata's primary aim is to establish scientific method (PDSA) thinking through habit. If the habit of PDSA becomes automatic or natural, then this will be a foundation for continuing improvement.

This is why it is called Kata – establishing the habit.

Establishing Kata aligns with the PDSA incremental experimental method. Rother defines management as *"the systematic pursuit of desired conditions by utilizing human capabilities in a concerted way"*. But Rother has been at pains to point out that Kata is not a tool but one of several ways to ingrain Lean behaviour. It is a teaching or learning routine. There are similarities with TWI, described in an earlier section. Habits were also described earlier.

In both Kata and TWI, skills are built up by repetition. Very often learners get it wrong for the first few times and need coaching. But confidence is built through feedback 'at the Gemba'. Hence there are unique improvement and leadership routines referred to by Rother as 'Improvement Kata' and 'Coaching Kata'.

There is the realistic assertion that one must have a target condition to know where one is going. With a target condition the direction and first few steps can be attempted. Very similar to the Agile approach to software development, one is not quite sure or confident about the overall path leading to achieving the target condition. So, one proceeds in small steps as with Scrum Sprints. These Sprints are experiments.

What is the first step? Try it. Does it move you closer? Reflect. Adjust. Avoid blame. What is now preventing us from moving ahead? What is the next specific small step to take? Don't think of some big, vague step like 'reduce inventory', but perhaps 'let us try running the workstation with a container of 8 parts rather than 10'. Not vague 'improve service' but try out a new method of answering queries. Small wins build confidence and motivation. Practice builds mindset. The habit is established with each 'que' of going to check.

Kata is effective because it is less threatening than 'big change' initiatives. Why not make the small, non-threatening changes as opportunities arise, coupled with experimentation, as suggested by Rother? He explains that whilst the 'target condition' might be known, the route to get there is uncertain. Many small steps, some of which will fail but from which we will learn, is the way to go. According to Rother *"Because the improvement kata is a set of behavioural guidelines, it is something that we learn through repeated practice. It takes conditioning to make behavioural routines become second nature, and consequently a lot of Toyota's managerial activities involve having people practise the improvement kata with their guidance."*

The **Improvement Kata** is a routine for moving from the current situation to a new situation in a creative, directed and meaningful way.

It has four elements:

1. Understand the direction
2. Grasp the current condition
3. Establish the next target condition. A measurable target.
4. PDSA toward the target condition

Then repeat and repeat again. This last step would often require several iterations, or PDSA cycles. Have patience.

Take one small step at a time and learn from each step. Don't try to take big steps, containing several smaller simultaneous steps. Why? Because some small steps will work but others may not –

but you may not be able to distinguish the successful from the unsuccessful if several initiatives are attempted at the same time. This is really the essence of the scientific method – set a hypothesis, test it, reject if necessary.

The **Coaching Kata** is a pattern for teaching the Improvement Kata. It is a set of coaching routines to practise in order to develop effective coaching habits.

It gives managers and supervisors a standardised approach to facilitate Improvement kata skill development in daily work. The Coaching Kata uses a standard set of five questions that are primarily focused on the leader or coach in an improvement area.

The five Coaching Kata Questions are:

1. What is the target condition? What is it we are trying to achieve?
2. What is the actual condition now?
3. What obstacles do you think are preventing you from reaching the target condition? Which one are you addressing now?
4. What is your next step? What do you expect to happen? (This is the start of the next PDSA cycle)
5. When can we go and see what we have learned from taking that step?

Feedback and review are integral to both Kata and Hoshin. Remember, Kata is a PDSA improvement cycle. Rother suggests that there are four 'Reflection Steps' for each small step carried out in an experimental cycle. The writers of this book believe that the Reflection Steps, if conscientiously carried out, are a principal benefit of Kata.

The four Reflection Steps are:

1. What did you plan as the last step?
2. What did you expect?
3. What actually happened?
4. What did you learn?

Sometimes there is a second coach, whose role is to make sure that the five steps and the four steps are followed, and to give guidance when they are not followed. Rother suggests these steps should form a daily 20-minute coaching cycle!

A few words of warning!

The Kata method is straightforward. That is a great attraction. But the practice is not so simple. Skill is required in each of the steps. Learning to ask the right 'small step' questions needs to be developed, again and again through deliberate practice.

Practice makes permanent

Do you do Karate (or perhaps some other martial art)? If so, you will know about 'Kata'. In a Kata, basic sequences are rehearsed even by high-Dan black belts. The actions establish and reinforce pathways in the brain and become automatic or a habit. This is important because when these skills are required in real life or competition, they are reproduced automatically. Many will have seen the famous sequence in the movie 'Karate Kid' with Mr. Miyagi: 'wax on, wax off'! All that repetition pays off as those skills become second nature when needed most.

A kata sequence is a way to learn. At first, you must obey the instructor exactly and without question. These are the basics that you simply must do correctly. Then, after you have mastered the basics, you don't need the instructor as regularly as before, and you can practice on your own, seeking perfection. You may sometimes add your own additions.

The final stage is where you have become so proficient that you can begin to instruct others. You often see this in martial arts classes where more experienced students take small groups of newer or younger students and give them instructions of the fundamental movements or actions.

Going through these stages will likely take you several years. A high-Dan Karate expert also seeks to develop an accompanying mental outlook. So, Kata can help develop both physically and mentally.

See for yourself

Let's try the four elements of the **Improvement Kata.** For example, you can improve your morning routine

- Understand the direction: what in your morning routine would you like to improve? Eating more healthily? Taking less time? Or....?
- Grasp the current condition: What are you doing now? And why?
- Establish the next target condition. A measurable target: Add one apple to your diet? How much less time? Or.....?
- PDSA toward the target condition. We tried the PDSA before. How can you use it here?

Further readings:

Rose Heathcote and Daryl Powell, *Improve Continuously by Mastering the Lean Kata*, The Lean Post, December 9, 2020

Mike Rother, *Toyota Kata*, McGraw Hill, 2010

Mike Rother, *The Toyota Kata Practice Guide*, McGraw Hill, 2017

Mike Rother and Gerd Aulinger, *Toyota Kata Culture*, McGraw Hill, 2017

Ideas and Suggestions

An **idea** is simply a **suggestion** (or thought or 'brainstorm') of a new or different way of doing something. Everyone has ideas almost every day, but what we are ideas that contribute to improved performance by people, products or services.

While all organisations integrate some form of idea or suggestion scheme into their business, the proposition put forward by Alan Robinson and Dean Schroeder in their book *"The Idea-Driven Organisation"* is that the organisation should be structured and aligned around idea generation. A surprising statistic by Robinson and Schroeder is that on average 80% of an organisation's performance improvement opportunity resides in front-line ideas, and only 20% in management focused initiatives. The notion that front-line improvements can outperform management initiatives by a factor of 4 to 1 is something that senior management teams find very hard to grasp. So why is this the case?

Idea generation can be push or pull, passive or pro-active. The classic passive type is the suggestion box. Generally, this only works for a while and later attracts cynical comments instead of suggestions. Non-acknowledgement and non-recognition have probably been the major reason for suggestion schemes producing poor results and being abandoned. If accepted, the idea is assigned to an individual or department for implementation which may result in further delay or unenthusiastic 'not-invented-here' attitude. Such systems are bureaucratic, slow and biased towards rejecting ideas. The results do not justify the time, hassle and overhead of running the system.

Yuso Yasuda has described the Toyota suggestion scheme or 'Kaizen system'. The scheme is co-ordinated by a 'creative idea suggestion committee' whose chairmanship has included Toyota chairmen (Toyoda and Saito) as well as Taiichi Ohno. Rewards for suggestions are given at Toyota based on a points system. Points are scored for tangible and intangible benefits, and for adaptability, creativity, originality, and effort. The rewards are invariably small amounts and are not based on a percentage of savings. However, operators value the token reward and the presentation ceremony itself. Note the contrast with typical Western Suggestion Schemes.

From the foregoing we learn a few important lessons:

- Not all improvements will pay, but creating the culture of improvement is more important.
- Give it time. The initial idea may be flawed, but developing the idea may prove a gold mine.
- Recognition is important - management cannot always be expected to give personal support, so establish a facilitator or function that can support.
- Do not underestimate potential opposition, especially from managers who may feel threatened by an idea.
- React rapidly to suggestions. Fully explain any idea rejections.
- Have a bias towards idea acceptance, not idea rejection.
- Give groups the tools and techniques, and the time

Unlike many western organisations Toyota don't adopt the "biggest bang for my buck" approach when it comes to idea generation. In fact, it is quite the opposite with a preference for the small incremental improvements. These of course will in time add up to significant change. Employees who come up with an improvement idea have to present it to their co-workers who will provide constructive feedback and encouragement. What's really significant is the coaching opportunity presented by the small ideas. The leader can get to understand the workers' thinking and logic, and where necessary point out any potential flaws. This helps to create an environment of trust where personal development and teamwork will flourish.

Are you open to a suggestion?

All of us have made suggestions to friends, or family, or colleagues about improving some aspect. Like taking a new route to work, recommending a show or movie, adding an ingredient to a cooked meal, painting a room, or reading a book. But what differs is how your suggestion was received. Was your suggestion enthusiastically accepted, rejected, shelved, ignored, or mocked? What was your response? Did it leave you feeling motivated and valued? Or disappointed and angry? (I'm never going to make a suggestion again!).

Some people are more receptive to suggestions than others. Some people are very sensitive to the way that suggestions are made! Also, some people making the suggestions seem to have an opinion and idea about everything everyone else is doing and feel compelled to speak up... It's a tricky balance, certainly when it comes communication.

See for yourself

Be alert to suggestions. Almost everyone makes suggestions.

- How do people respond? Are they positive? Are you?
- Why do you think some people respond negatively to suggestions? What do you think would be a better way to communicate ideas to family or friends, or at work?
- Make a list of guidelines to be followed with ideas. For instance, include response time, displays, and coping with rejections. Now compare your list with guidelines in your organisation, if any. Now What suggestions do you have about making suggestions?
- At work, do you think there is a reluctance to put forward ideas? Are you or your colleagues fearful of putting forward ideas? This is the psychological safety. 'Drive out fear', said Deming. Re-read the Learning section on toleration of mistakes.

Further readings:

Andy Brophy and John Bicheno, *Innovative Lean*, PICSIE Books, 2010 (This contains details of several Idea Management Systems, and concepts for Idea generation.)

Alan Robinson and Dean Schroeder, *The Idea Driven Organisation*, Berrett-Koehler, 2014

Yuzo Yasuda, 40 Years, *20 Million Ideas*, Productivity, 1990

Coaching

Coaching is a form of development in which an experienced person, called a coach, supports a learner or client in achieving a specific personal or professional goal by providing training and guidance.

One of the most critical tasks leaders at all levels in organisations face today is in assisting their subordinates to achieve their full potential. A key component in making this happen is the leader's ability to develop coaching skills that can release their employee's capability in a structured, safe environment. In fact, according to Mike Rother (*Toyota Kata*, 2018) coaching has become so critical in developing both individuals and organisations, that it is likely to become a significant factor in career progression and consequently a subject at business schools.

While coaching encompasses many activities and techniques borrowed from other disciplines such as counselling, psychology, education, and consulting it is best defined by Whitmore (1992) who suggests that: *"Coaching is unlocking people's potential to maximise their own performance."*

Lean coaching is a fundamental requirement in creating an environment where sustainable continuous improvement can take hold and thrive. In a Lean coaching relationship, the coach will ask questions that stimulate critical thinking skills and reinforce systematic approaches for improving how leaders lead, and how work is done.

An important point is that coaching allows empowerment, participation, and delegation. Why? Because coaching your team, allows them to take on more responsibility. This is exactly in line with the Lean concept of 'creating thinking people'. So, coaching should be done by every Lean manager, not by the HR function.

Lean coaches are often referred to as a sensei. A Lean sensei is a master teacher of Lean tools, systems and principles. A sensei is more focused on facilitating and teaching Lean thinking than on the tools. A Lean sensei typically stands outside of an organization, allowing him or her objectively to see what needs to be done and to develop a true continuous improvement culture without having to worry about internal politics or strong personalities.

In Michael Bungay Stanier's excellent book *The Coaching Habit* (a book that every aspiring Lean Manager should have) he gives a series of open questions beginning with 'What's on your mind?', followed by 'and what else?'. The questions are not a strict series but often involve cycling back to probe further. Resist giving your 'solution' but instead ask about the challenge. Remember, every time you give a 'solution' you are preventing someone from making it themselves! Which is likely to have greater acceptance – their idea or your idea?

Another question is particularly interesting for fans of the '5 Whys' (Root Cause Analysis). Stanier suggests asking 'What' instead of 'Why', particularly when followed by 'did you...'. Following this, comes the next question: 'How can I help?' Throughout this process, never underestimate silence and listening. The Quakers have a tactic that has been used to good effect for 350 years - if there is a disagreement, then 'let's just have 2 minutes silence'.

A powerful different perspective

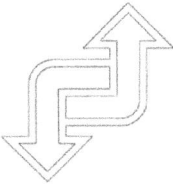

Many will be familiar with a sports coach, say in football or tennis. Perhaps you have experience yourself of being a sports coach.

Of course, there are professional coaches but you probably have been a coach yourself in helping friends, fellow students, or family by putting forward suggestions aimed at helping based on your own experience or expertise. The fact that you were not labelled as a coach is not important, coaching is the activity, not the title. And conversely, you are likely to have received 'coaching' from others including parents. They ask questions, offer guidance and suggestions for you to make corrections and improvements, based on their experience and perspective.

See for yourself

Reflect on the situations above. What makes 'coaching' effective, and when and why is it appreciated, or resented?

- We have all been coached (or given advice) at some time or other, at various stages in our life and by various people. What circumstances were most memorable? Who had significant influence?

Further readings:

Michael Bungay Stanier, *The Coaching Habit*, Box of Crayons Press, 2016. Note: Access the web site www.boxofcrayons.com for several resources

John Whitmore, *Coaching for Performance*, Nicholas Bearley, 2017

Sprint retrospective

A **sprint retrospective** is a meeting held at the end of each iteration (sprint) in Scrum.

Scrum is an Agile method used in software development and in other industries. Its purpose is to reflect on the previous sprint's performance, identify areas for improvement, and plan actions for better results. Topics discussed may include process improvements, team dynamics, tools, and metrics. By evaluating these aspects, teams can adapt their methods and continuously improve.

A Sprint retrospective has:

- **Participants:** Team members involved in the project, including developers, product owners, scrum masters, designers, and testers.
- **Goal:** To inspect and adapt the team's processes, methods, and behaviours to improve the next sprint's outcome.
- **Format:** Typically follows a structured format, such as:
    - Start with a round-robin discussion, where each participant shares their thoughts on what went well, what didn't, and suggestions for improvement
    - Identify common themes or areas of improvement based on the team's feedback
    - Agree on specific actions to address these areas and assign responsibilities
    - Set concrete goals and timelines for implementing these changes

Common topics discussed during sprint retrospectives include:

- **Process improvements:** Refining workflows, streamlining tasks, or adjusting communication channels
- **Team dynamics:** Addressing conflicts, fostering collaboration, or improving cross-functional understanding

- **Tools and technologies:** Evaluating the effectiveness of specific software tools or hardware used in the project
- **Metrics and tracking:** Reviewing performance indicators to identify areas for improvement

The sprint retrospective is an essential component of Scrum's iterative approach, as it helps teams learn from their experiences, adapt to challenges, and continuously improve their processes.

Further readings:

Marjolijn Feringa and Jeroen Venneman, *Agile FOCUS in governance*, 2020, Van Haren Publishing

---

After Action Reviews (AARs)

After Action Reviews are post-activity assessments used to improve and learn from events. The goal is to avoid repeating mistakes and to continuously learn and improve.

AARs are now becoming widespread. AARs originated in the military (for example the 'Top Gun' school – have you seen the movie?). There is a great deal of similarity with Coaching and with Sprint Retrospectives, and with PDSA.

The characteristics of AAR's are:

- They are done routinely after every part project, Sprint, Lean improvement, football match, or lecture session.
- A good facilitator (not the leader), is needed who follows the rules below.
- It is done immediately after the action, or as soon as possible thereafter.
- Use objective data only. What was the aim, and what exactly was done?
- Participation: As far as possible all should attend, including all managers. Of course, there are practical group size limitations. A dozen people?

- Status and hierarchy are downplayed. Subordinates should feel free to express views without threat. (Psychological safety).
- Start by asking the team members (NOT the leader) the questions below. But...
- No personal criticism is allowed. *What* happened, not *who*.
- Leaders should be willing to admit that mistakes were made.
- It is an opportunity for all to reflect and then to learn, via a learning cycle.
- A time limit. 30 minutes (or less) ? The late David Garvin of Harvard Business School suggests time is spent approximately; What did we set out to do and What actually happened: (together 25%); Why did it happen that way (25%); What should be done next time / What would be better (50%)
- Garvin's studies reveal that AARs fail when not following the above characteristics or rules, with a big issue being the willingness of seniors to admit that they got it wrong.

How did the match go?

A lot of people play football and are maybe even serious about it. It may not be professional football, but it is still an serious game for lots of players. During the season, playing a match every week and it is customary to have a match review after the match.

The coach shows footage of the match and situations he noticed. Sometimes they are things that went very well, sometimes there are areas for improvement. By seeing and analysing this together as a team, you come to agreements for the next match and pick up certain things that will be practised extra in training. The match review is also a time when all players get the opportunity to share their opinions on certain things.

See for yourself

How did your day go? Reflect on it. Did you meet your goals? What would you have done differently. What are you proud of? Does the reflection change your plans for tomorrow?

- If not already doing something similar, try suggesting doing an AAR with your lecturer, your manager, your coach. Use the guidelines above.

Further readings:

Anders Eriksson, *Peak*, Bodley Head, 2016

David Garvin, *Learning in Action*, Harvard, 2000

Motivating and Measuring

How to get traction?

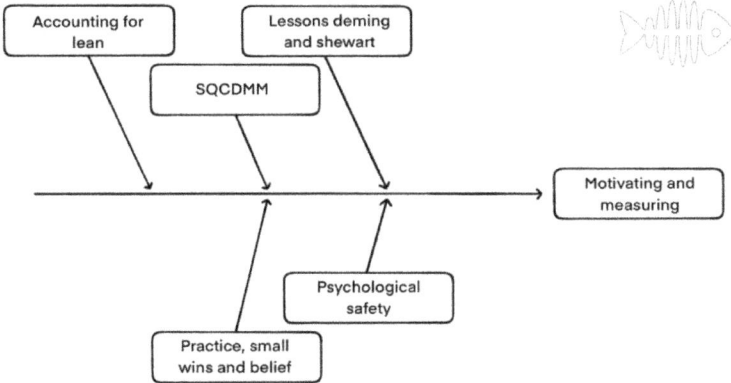

Back to the bike...

It's nice to know that all our effort and hard work is paying off. Knowing how well we're doing means we need to measure our progress or performance. *But for our journey, what should we measure? Do we measure cadence, speed, distance travelled, or heart rate? Do we measure key destinations past at particular*

times? Do we measure how happy or tired we are? Or how costly our bikes are?

We need to measure the right things, and we need to be willing and able to use this information to stay focused, stay energised, and adjust when required.

- How do we know what to measure and if this is helping us on our journey?
- How do we measure in a way that we can recognise improvements?
- How do we create a safe environment where everyone can be at their best?

Motivating and measuring are closely linked and comprise many concepts some of which are given in the fishbone. Lean and Agile have key lessons that can help us make this possible.

Accounting for Lean

Lean Accounting is an accounting method that tries to minimise the number of transactions and the increase the efficiency of the accounting process.

Accounting for Lean is the prime way in which the financial aspects of Lean and Agile are measured. It is an accounting philosophy that tries to improve decision making within the accounting process to enable and facilitate Lean operations.

First of all, one needs to distinguish between 'Lean Accounting', and 'Accounting for Lean'.

Ultimately both have a common purpose: To track only the relevant financial information that helps drive further Lean activity with minimal transactions and maximum efficiency.

As Ohno is reported to have said, 'Costs do not exist to be calculated; costs exist to be reduced.' Therefore, much of cost accounting is waste; but cost reduction is not waste.

David Cochrane, Thomas Johnson and John Seddon, amongst others, have made the point that many companies are now managed the wrong way around. They start with measures or targets, then work out the physical solutions (the 'hows' and the 'whats'). By contrast, becoming Lean should start with the purpose, derive 'hows' and 'whats', and then choose to reinforce achievement. As Deming pointed out, managers should not use financial targets to control financial results, instead, manage the relationships that produce these results.

Accounting for Lean is a developing field. So, what should Accounting for Lean give us?

- More relevant information for decision-making. More relevant means the ability to identify factors and products that are becoming uncompetitive, and where there are potential opportunities for improvement.
- Positive support and evidence for doing the right things – fast, flexible, flow. For reducing inventories and lead times, for improving quality, and for improving delivery performance.
- Financial numbers that are able to be understood by non-accountants without having to go through several days of education. Develop 'Plain English' profit and loss statements that exclude variances, show actual operations profit, and have additional lines that show changes in overhead, labour and inventory.
- A simplified system that cuts waste and unnecessary transactions. A Lean accounting system needs to be a minimalist system – tracking only the absolute minimum transactions with the lowest frequency possible.
- A system that highlights when to take action, as importantly when not to.
- Guidance on medium term product costing and target costing.

Finally, Ohno said that an aim of TPS should be to make the system so simple and visible that there would be little need for complex controls. Ohno also said: *'Excess information must be supressed'*. Visual controls should largely suffice. So real Lean should aim at cutting overheads!

Mindlessly Measuring

Most people keep track of their money – the inputs and outputs, their debts, their savings, and the ability to pay for aspirations such as a holiday or a house.

But how is this done? Some make budgets, some keep spreadsheets, others keep a written record. Or combinations of these. And some just 'muddle through'. Very likely you will want to keep track of the amount of money spent per day, and per week. And are you on plan or off plan? This is a matter of personal choice. But, probably, few use full double entry bookkeeping with full budgets and variances calculated regularly by category. Why? To do so may be thought necessary for some businesses but for individuals this is 'over the top'. All you need are the essentials, nothing extra. Remember, 'cash is king'.

The same sort of question arises with Lean. Although Financial Accounting may be a requirement, detailed cost accounting needs review if it is to achieve the aims given above. It needs to be just sufficient for purpose. Moreover, there are accounting conventions that can lead to decisions that conflict with Lean. For example, inventory is considered an asset in conventional accounting, but should be minimised in a Lean environment. Absorption costing can encourage overproduction if overheads are apportioned by product volume. If you use standard costing and have a new kitchen installed, you may not be able to afford to eat at home because the cost of the kitchen has to be apportioned amongst the meals you prepare!

SQCDMMS

SQCDMMS is an acronym for a set of measure categories widely used in Lean organisations and displayed at each line or area.

These measures allow teams to be focused on the right activities and track progress against an agreed cross-functional plan. SQCDMMS was mentioned in the Visual Management section. Making the measures visible and accessible is important.

The categories are:

- **Safety** comes first. Accidents, Unsafe acts and audit of unsafe conditions. (For more on this, please refer to the People Fishbone.)
- **Quality**. Internal scrap, rework, and first time through – expressed in parts per million. 'First time through' percentage is 'parts entering minus parts scrapped or reworked at each stage'. Because rework can happen several times this measure can be negative. But Quality is also to do with the far wider consideration of customer satisfaction. See below. After Safety, this should be a prime aim of measurement.
- **Cost.** Costs are important of course because costs that are too high will drive any organisation out of existence. Cost can be a productivity measure – units per person per week.
- **Delivery performance.** Inbound from suppliers, outbound to customers. QOTIF: Quality, On Time in Full. The higher the percentage of on time in full delivered by the supplier, the higher the score. And the higher the QOTIF for customers, the higher will be their satisfaction.
- **Morale.** Absenteeism, suggestions or improvements are indicators of high or low morale. Possibly make use of an attitude audit.
- **Management.** Communications, extent of cross training, attendance at shop floor meetings.

Arguably, there are four basic or prime measures for Lean. Each of them encourages 'all the right moves'. Each can be implemented on various levels from cell to plant, even supply chain. They are also a set, to be looked at together:

1. **Lead time:** Measuring lead-time encourages inventory reduction, one-piece flow, reduction of flow length, and

waste reduction. The measure is best done end-to-end from the receiving dock to dispatch. Next best is to track only 'work in process' lead-time. A variation on this measure is to track 'Ohno's Time Line' – the time between receiving an order and receiving payment, expressed in $ per hour. This is particularly good since it includes transaction processing time and puts the emphasis on cash flow.

2. **Customer Satisfaction:** Following the first Lean principle, monitoring customers is a basic requirement. If failure is indicated here, this must be the first priority. It is important to get this measure from customers, not internally from shipments or marketing. An obvious question is – who are your customers? Final or intermediate? Answer: Both. Sample them across all relevant dimensions – cost, quality, delivery as basics, but note also soft measures such as the RATER framework: reliability, assurance, tangibles, empathy, responsiveness. (See Zeithaml and Bitner, *Services Marketing*, 2006).

3. **Schedule Attainment:** An internal measure of consistency. Schedule attainment is the ability to hit the target for quantity and quality on a day-to-day basis, line-by-line, or cell-by-cell – not weekly for the plant. Again, track the distribution. Compare the best with the worst, and seek opportunities - not blame. If you have a Heijunka system this is straightforward. Of course, if the schedule is out of line with customer demands, the measure is a waste of time.

4. **Inventory Turns, and 'SWIP to WIP':** Inventory turns is an established measure. An alternative is days of inventory. Better is to break it down into raw material, WIP, and finished goods days. Why? Because WIP is fully under your own control, raw materials and finished goods are not fully under own control. SWIP is standard work in progress inventory, so measuring the variation between what should be and actual, is useful.

How am I really doing?

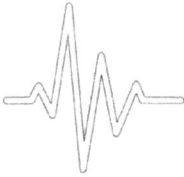

How do you measure and monitor yourself? For example, your weight or maybe your heart rate? Maybe you track your physical activities (minutes per week) or your strength (kg/reps/sets)?

What about how you manage your finances? The amount of money spent per day, and per week? Are you on plan or off plan? What types of things did you spend it on?

How about your behaviours? How many hours are you on your phone, watching TV or perhaps gaming? How many alcoholic drinks do you consume each week? How much is too much? Is this number growing? Do you have warnings or limits for these activities?

Do you have balance in your life where the critical items to measure are sustainable and supporting you in improving?

How can you tell? Do you record data (calories eaten, steps walked, hours slept, money spent etc) and how do you track it? Is it graphically and visually? Perhaps an app or timer? Do you use this information to notice trends and perhaps correlations in behaviours?

Do you do this regularly and consistently? Measures are far more effective when monitored regularly. Sometimes we forget to pay closer attention to what is really going on in our life. By paying attention to measures that matter, we can be on the front foot when it comes to being at our best.

See for yourself

What do you measure in your life? Your weight? Your heartrate? Reflect on it. For instance, do you measure how long it takes to get to work? Some men always measure their biceps. Are these measurements the things you find most important or are there different things that you should be measuring?

- These days many smart watches enable you to measure yourself and your activities automatically. Your fitness? Your heart rate? Your cardio? Sleep patterns? Calories burned? Your exercise? Your stand frequency? Which do you monitor and why? Does this, or has this, made a difference to your daily activities?

Lessons from Deming and Shewhart

W. Edwards Deming (1900 – 1993) is widely recognised as a one of the fathers of quality management but also as a significant management philosopher and statistician. He is so highly respected that part of his legacy is *The Deming Prize* which is Japan's top-quality award. Deming had and has a huge influence on Lean thinking.

Walter A. Shewhart was Deming's mentor early in his career and had a major influence on his work and contributions.

Deming became famous for his writings and teachings and leaves a significant body of theories, principles, and philosophies. There is still much to learn from his work and so here we partly summarise some of his most well-known material:

- Some of his **'14 points for Management'**.
- His system of **'Profound knowledge'**.
- His **'94/6 Rule'**.

Of course, there is much more to Deming than just these, and reading his work is recommended.

Demings 14 Points for Management

This is a series of principles for management to follow to improve the effectiveness of a business or organization significantly.

Whilst all 14 are valuable, below some of particular relevance have been summarised:

- A consistent message is necessary to create a shared understanding by all in the system, of what principles drive decision making.
- A commitment to continuously improve as a system, not isolated pockets of improvement activity.
- Prevention of quality issues is always superior to the detection of them.
- Avoid awarding business based on price. Go for longer term partnerships built on collaboration, loyalty, and trust.
- Use the scientific method (PDSA). Decisions for improvement should be based on relevant objective data and reasoning.
- 'Drive out fear'- create an environment where people feel safe enough to share honest reporting about system performance.
- Avoid slogans to communicate the focus of your improvement. Slogans are often focussed on a particular target, as opposed to systematic change.

Demings Profound Knowledge

This is a highly integrated framework of thought and action for any leader wishing to transform an organization. This system has four practices that, according to him, are widely misunderstood or ignored by managers. As a result, they are the root causes of many organisational problems. The four practices are:

1. Appreciation of system (thinking). The system contains interrelated connections and interactions working together for a shared aim.
2. Scientific method. The use of hypotheses, experiments, and evidence to support data driven decision making.
3. Understanding of variation. Recognising its two types (arrival and process) and understanding their

causes enables behaviour to be predicted, problems resolved, and improvements to be made.
4. Extrinsic rewards are at best only short-term. Seek intrinsic rewards ('joy in work'). Create a system where people take pride in what they do.

Demings 94/6 Rule

Deming's belief is that 94% of problems are caused by the system, and only 6% by people. Yet, the default mode is to first blame the person. Deming said: 'A bad system will beat a good person every time'. Hence, managers 'learn' never to praise 'good' performance, but always to criticise 'poor' performance! Demotivating and misleading!

No matter how well you measure a person's performance, ultimately, they will be undermined by a poor performing system.

By focusing on improving the overall work environment, or value stream, and not focusing on individual measures for employees, the system as a whole can improve.

A quotation from W Edwards Deming's famous book, Out of the Crisis, serves as a salutary warning on measures: 'Rates for production are often set to accommodate the average worker. Naturally, half of them are above average, and half below. What happens is that peer pressure holds the upper half to the rate, and no more. The people below the average cannot make the rate. The result is loss, chaos, dissatisfaction, and turnover.'

Deming illustrated his frustration with managers and measures with his famous red bead game. Six volunteers draw 50 beads at a time from a container having red and white beads, using a paddle. The reds represent defects. The participants are urged to produce fewer defects. Of course there is variation between the participants, but it is out of their control. The 'good' performers are praised, the 'bad' ones given a warning. Some improve ('so giving a warning works!'), but some don't, and are fired. 'Managers don't understand variation', said Deming. Do you?

This amusing game nicely illustrates 'regression to the mean'. If you get a high reading this time, there is a very good chance that you will get a lower reading next time. And a low reading will very likely be followed by a high reading. Hence, managers 'learn' never to praise 'good' performance, but always to criticise 'poor' performance.

Shewhart's Insight

Shewhart, Deming's teacher, saw measurement having three elements, the data, the human observer, and the conditions. Note that all three are subject to variation.

However, these three sources of variation are often ignored. We tend to use the average, whilst ignoring variation. There is a vast difference between performance with small variation and performance with high variation, even though the latter may have a slightly better average.

Everyone filters (or interprets) data according to their own bias and background. We all implicitly use models, mental or written, good or bad – and they are uncertain. Since we are dealing with uncertainties in data, in observation, and interpretation we should use control charts to assist in understanding the variation – whether special cause or common cause.

See for yourself

Have a think about your own daily activities, perhaps where you work, or how you operate at home. What do you think about the following statements?

- Monetary incentives are effective.
- Fear motivates.
- Most problems are due to people.
- Variation is inconsequential in management, or to management.
- Quality is the responsibility of the Quality Department.

- Suppliers should be judged and chosen on price.
- Short term profits are what counts.
- Defect prevention is more important than defect detection.
- Scientific method for improvement is not necessary.

Find some fellow freshers and spend some time discussing these statements above. What are your ideas and conclusions?

The Performance Trilogy (Practice, Small Wins, Belief)

Practice is defined as the act of doing something repeatedly or regularly with the aim to improve or master a particular skill or behaviour. The willingness to use constructive feedback is a critical factor in the progressive improvement in performance.

These progressions in performance over time accumulate as **Small Wins**, leading to large wins. Large step changes in performance are unusual. However, many stable, but consistent improvements with feedback have a powerful impact on motivation. **Belief** on the part of a person and belief of a manager in their people is necessary. The manager gives constructive feedback, recognises and gives credit for small wins, and allows practice for skills to develop.

For good human performance three interacting characteristics are necessary: Practice, Small Wins, and Belief. The three work together. Omitting one risks failure.

Practice

People learn work skills over time with deliberate practice, small wins, and with a belief mindset – not only in the person but within the wider organisation. Repetition is insufficient; coaching and feedback are required.

Yes, talent is important, but without practice, and encouragement it will be insufficient.

Small Wins

Recent years have revealed the power of small and 'varied wins' motivation. In a seminal 1984 article, Karl Weick said; *'By itself, one small win may seem unimportant. A series of small wins at small but significant tasks, however, reveals a pattern that may attract allies, deter opponents, and lower resistance to subsequent proposals. Small wins are controllable opportunities that produce visible results. Once a small win has been accomplished, forces are set in motion that favour another small win. When a solution is put in place, the next solvable problem often becomes more visible. This occurs because new allies bring new solutions with them and old opponents change their habits.'* (A crucial quote for Lean transformation!)

More recently, Teresa Amabile and Steven Kramer's momentous work at Harvard Business School has elaborated on the power of small wins on 'positive inner work life'. Small wins are shown to be most powerful motivating factor, but need to be supported with 'catalysts' (for instance clear goals, and providing resources and time) and 'nourishers' (for instance, respect, and encouragement).

Remember that progress is non-linear. There will be setbacks. But the question is, what was learned from the setbacks?

Belief

During these setbacks, there sometimes needs to be more than just the evidence of small progression to fall back on. There needs to be the belief that what we are aiming at and trying to achieve is actually possible and we are on the right track. Belief can underpin motivation, when progress takes a slight knock, or even at the very start, belief that something currently impossible, is possible.

A Trilogy of Possibility

If you are trying to improve performance in any sport (say swimming, running, karate, football) you need a trilogy of approaches. First, you need **Practice** through repetition. The best sportspeople practice and practice and practice. Not just mindless practice, but deliberate practice. It's not much good to practice if you are making the same mistakes with your style over and over again. Deliberate practice means being observed, receiving constructive feedback, then correcting and improving your style.

After this comes the **Small Wins**, consistently achieving a succession of small gains. First, run 100m in 20 seconds, then 19, then 18, then 17.5, and so on. Small wins encourage further small wins and reinforce deliberate practice.

But all this must be done with **Belief**, not only in yourself but also by your mentor or coach. This last is a 'mindset thing'. The psychologist Carol Dwek says that there are two types of mindset – fixed mindset and growth mindset. A growth mindset has a desire to learn and is based on the belief that intelligence can be developed. This is associated with Dwek's famous word, 'YET'. So, not that you *can't* do mathematics (that would be a fixed mindset), but that you can't do mathematics YET. That Belief on the part of a leader is necessary is no longer in dispute. For instance, Nobel psychologist Daniel Kahneman showed this with Israeli army recruits. Leaders were told that one group was superior and another average. Both groups were randomly selected, but at the end of training the 'superior' group really was better!

The trilogy applies to individuals and to teams. It also applies to learning – learning a language, learning to play a musical instrument, or learning any academic discipline.

See for yourself

This also applies in day-to-day activities such as learning to cook, or fix and repair items around the house. Choose one of the examples or create your own.

- What can you practise, can you create small wins?
- When you achieve a small win, what does that do for you confidence?
- Look at the section below on Demand and Shewhart. Deming's Red Bead Game is discussed. Could this apply to belief in leaders? Has this been relevant to your experience?

Psychological Safety

Psychological safety is the belief that it is safe to speak up, to question, to make mistakes, to ask for help, and to take risks. All without interpersonal fear of humiliation, rejection, or punishment.

Psychological Safety is eliminating the fear of punishment or sanction resulting from expressing an opinion or idea that 'seniors' may not like. 'Drive our fear' said the quality guru W Edwards Deming. Or from George Orwell, 'If liberty means anything at all, it means the right to tell people what they do not want to hear.' It allows people to be at their best and to be authentic in their words and actions. It promotes and releases individual and group potential, as well as an environment for growth and improved performance.

Psychological safety has some important features:

- **Making people feel safe and secure** – as in a family. Everyone is included. Excluding a person from a group (deliberate or not) has been shown to have severe psychological consequences. Respect implies inclusivity.
- **Fostering work as a learning, growing process.**

- **A willingness to admit mistakes**. This works two ways: humility from top down, and confidence and security from bottom up. Pulling the Andon cord with confidence. Thomas Watson (IBM founder) and his famous reaction to an employee who made a $1m mistake: 'Fire you? Of course not! I have just invested $1m in your education.'
- **Replacing blame with curiosity.**
- **Openness and accessibility.** The boss who spends time on the shop floor; not to inspect and criticise, but as a person who is there to help and learn.
- **The analogy of the 'Hot Stove Rule'.** A family gathers around the hot stove. Support, help and encouragement (warmth) is given. If a transgression occurs (touching the stove) instant discipline is administered (burn) but the stove has no memory and continues to give warmth.

For improving Psychological Safety we draw on the excellent work of Amy Edmondson for inspiration. Briefly, active work is required for all the following:

- **Purpose.** What, exactly, is the expected response with respect to mistakes, accidents, and safety?
- **Structure.** What needs to be reported and what doesn't? The ease and speed of communicating mistakes.
- **Understanding, responding and not over-reacting**, to mistakes that are predictable, preventable, complex, and an 'intelligent mistake'. Classify those that one can learn from, and those that need to be fixed. Standards that need to be followed, and standards that can be questioned. The time frames for expected responses require consideration.
- **Personal security.** Attitudes to mistakes and to being wrong.
- **Behaviour.** Clarify the types of behaviour that will always be supported, and the types of 'mistakes' that will get you fired. (e.g. Sexist remarks). Whistleblowing policy?
- **Active listening.** Listen attentively and provide appropriate responses

- **Discouraging and surfacing workarounds.** A workaround may gain 'brownie points' but they result in problems and mistakes being overlooked – or, worse, encouraged.
- **Being Humble**. Diminish rank and status, or signs of self-importance.
- **Overcoming the 'Sounds of Silence'** (to quote Simon and Garfunkel). Methods include round-robin speaking opportunity at meetings, and direct asking.
- **Voice.** The choice of words used in an organisation with respect to mistakes is influential to actions. Words need to be consistent and unambiguous within the organisation. A mistake or an error? A failure or an accident? A stoppage or an opportunity? A A deviation or a defect? A nuisance and a 'screw-up'?
- **Appreciation and acknowledgement of mistakes** that have been surfaced.

Finally, a quote from Pfeffer and Sutton: *"The implication is that leaders need to make a fundamental decision: Do they want to be told they are always right, or do they want to lead organisations that actually perform well?"*

Safe Enough to Speak?

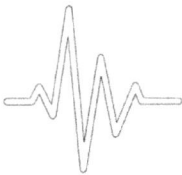

You operate in multiple environments day to day. It may be the family home. It may be a full or a part time job. Perhaps you are in some form of education or work closely with your management team or colleagues.

Think about your own psychological safety?

Do you always feel safe enough to ask questions, to check information, to try something never done without feeling embarrassed or ridiculed? Do you feel safe enough to take risks and potentially fail, or do you feel unsafe, and prioritise avoiding failure. Do you behave in a way that isn't authentic due to the response and perception of others?

Are you scared to voice your opinion? That your questions are seen as an attack and in some way feel punished for asking them? What about contributions you know you can make, but don't feel would be heard?

All these questions lead us to understand and be aware of how psychologically safe our environment is, and what needs to change to allow everyone to release their potential.

This subject is closely linked with the earlier section on ideas and suggestions, but having much wider relevance and applicability.

See for yourself

Think back at a time you felt really safe and think back at a time you did not. What differences did you feel inside yourself? How did you behave differently? What did you see others do? What would you do different now?

Further readings:

Amy Edmondson, *Right Kind of Wrong: Why Learning to fail can teach us to thrive, Cornerstone Press*, 2023

Adam Grant, *Think Again*, WH Allen, 2021

Problem Solving

How to find and fix.

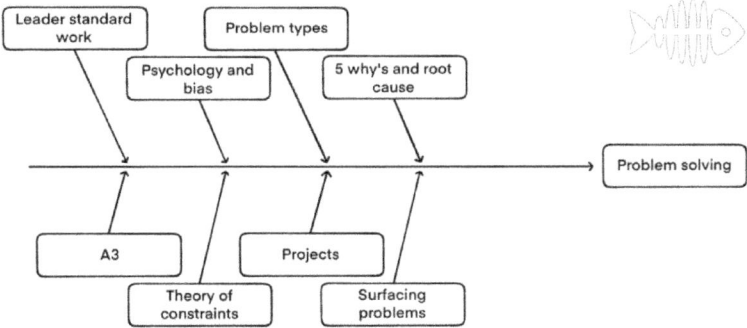

On your bike...

We need to accept that we're going to bump into some problems along the way, in fact, it is better to actively look for the problem before it shows its head. Perhaps fatigue, dangerous traffic, cycling effectively as a group, and staying on plan? If not, issues quickly turn into problems, incidents inevitably to accidents.

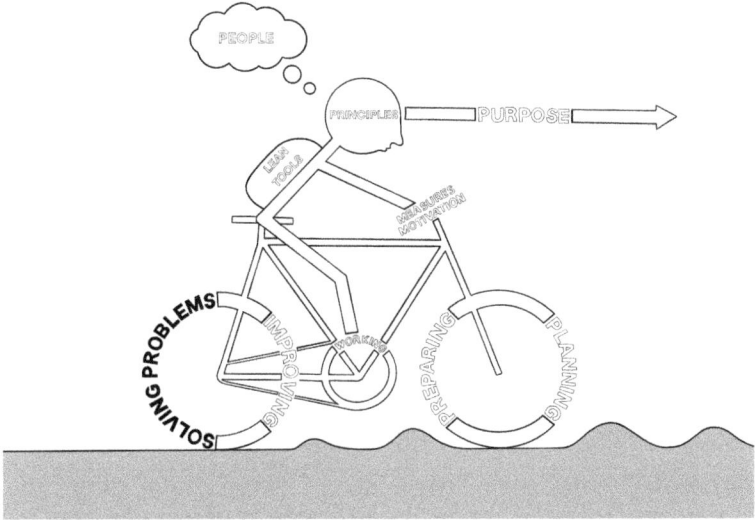

- Are we staying alert so we can recognise and deal with problems effectively?
- Is everyone following the rules of the road? How do we make sure?
- What is the real cause of the issues we could, or have faced?
- What is restricting us from moving consistently at the same pace?
- If we have a particular problem, do we know how best to respond?

You can't fix something you can't find. Effective problem solving requires us to know how to look for, how to recognise, and how to respond to problems.

To be Lean and Agile, is to understand what plays a part in both 'finding', and 'fixing'.

To begin, let us make two general points:

1. Taiichi Ohno said, "Having no problems is the biggest problem of all.". All systems have problems inherent within them. To 'not have a problem' may suggest not recognising, not acknowledging, or even worse, hiding problems that are inhibiting desired performance.
2. The second point comes from the Nobel prize winner, Daniel Kahneman in his wonderful book *Thinking, Fast and Slow*. According to Kahneman, the human brain has two modes of thinking:
   - **System 1:** This thinking is intuitive, it operates automatically and quickly, with little or no effort or voluntary control.
   - **System 2:** Deliberately allocates attention and effort to mental activities and complex computations that demand it.

These points are illustrated in the passage below:

A by-now famous question developed by Shane Frederick of Yale University, is 'A bat and a ball cost $1.10 in total. The bat costs

$1.00 more than the ball. How much does the ball cost?' A very high proportion of people (irrespective of education) give the incorrect answer of $0.10. This is System 1 thinking. When using System 2 thinking you will come to the right answer: $0.05. Try this out yourself and experience the difference.

This is illustrative of the danger of using quick-response, intuitive answers. Quick response, or System 1 Thinking is one of the greatest barriers to good problem solving. This is because System 1 contains some 'systematic errors'. It is prone to bias in certain circumstances, and as it runs automatically, you can't turn it off. System 1 is appropriate in emergency situations, but is too often used in response to criticism, a challenge to status, or the desire to be thought of as decisive. System 2 thinking, by contrast, is slow, deliberate, and logical. Therefore, effective problem solvers should get into the habit of taking a moment, taking a breath, taking some seconds of silence, whilst reflecting on the wider issues involved.

Throughout this Chapter, we discuss how who we are and how we solve problems are inextricably linked. Understanding this, leads us to be more effective in how we 'find and fix'.

Leader Standard Work

Leader Standard Work (LSW) is the documented and current best way to do a particular task, procedure, or process. It is a set of consistent behaviours and recurring activities that advances a Continuous Improvement culture.

LSW applies the same concept as an employee's standard work, but with the focus on driving Lean thinking and behaviour throughout the organisation. LSW work involves drawing up a timetable of activities each leader in the organization, from team leader to Vice President, needs to follow to assist in driving improvement.

The practice also incorporates coaching and mentoring opportunities, and surfaces immediate opportunities to improve processes. Through LSW, leaders get to understand what is working well, what isn't, and where change is necessary. LSW is closely related to the 'Gemba' concept. Of course, a 'Leader' is not necessarily the CEO or COO. A leader could be a team leader, a departmental leader, or a value stream co-ordinator.

Specifically, LSW is a system to support leaders in:

- Focusing on the critical tasks/activities.
- Defining and exhibiting ideal behaviours and mentoring and coaching their people.
- Recognising employees for their commitment and performance.
- Engaging with their employees to understand the issues that affect them in performing their daily work and displaying a "Lead by Humility" approach.
- Demonstrating their commitment to employee engagement.
- Structuring and prioritising their tasks and activities.
- Managing their time efficiently.

In his excellent book, *Creating a Lean Culture*, David Mann says that there are four principal elements of Lean Management:

1. LSW.
2. Visual controls.
3. Daily Accountability Process.
4. Leadership Discipline.

Of these, LSW has the 'highest leverage' and helps consolidate the other three.

Maasaki Imai created a famous diagram on how people spend their time in a Kaizen organisation. It shows the proportion of time spent on Kaizen activity decreasing with every increase in an employee's management level. (See the earlier section on Kaizen.) Of course, a senior manager is extremely busy and may spend only a little time regularly on LSW, but it should never be zero!

Some useful guidelines to assist leaders in their behaviours and activities are:

- Every management layer supports and audits the layer and the process below it.
- LSW should form part of regular 1-1 conversations.
- The process is the main focus, not only the result.
- LSW should be concentrated on improving the process and supporting the people.

However:

- While LSW helps to establish and sustain a particular leadership style across the organisation, it does reduce leaders' discretion. Some leaders may not like this.
- LSW requires considerable discipline, failure to be consistent can send the wrong message about commitment.
- LSW should be reviewed and updated on a regular basis for new standards based on improvements.

A variation on LSW is to use 'leaders' to audit a selection of standard work procedures. This is done at the Gemba and is standard practice at Toyota plants. Perhaps a senior manager would do an audit once a month, a department leader once a fortnight, and a section leader once per week. What they would look for is an associate's ability not only to follow the standard steps, but also their knowledge of key points and the reasons for those key points. A 'Job Breakdown Sheet' may be used by the leader for the task. This task not only clearly demonstrates the importance of Standard Work but also builds an understanding by leaders of the steps within their processes.

So... tell me about your day

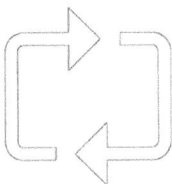

In the previous Chapter we talked about Gemba Walks with the example of parents actively engaging and enquiring as to the current situation family members in the house are in. Actually going to the persons room or study area, asking 'how are things going' is better than a meeting held in a general room.

LSW adds structure and consistency to this approach. Perhaps a daily routine of being visible in specified areas, asking about specific critical tasks (homework deadlines, sports events), perhaps a board in the kitchen as to who is doing what and when.

Being 'curious and interested' about issues, progress, help and support – let's not forget praise! This consistency and structure sends a powerful message, "I know things have to be done routinely and to a standard, but I can see I am also being supported in doing so".

Now perhaps imagine grandparents and their weekly visit. I'm sure they have a few questions for the parents as well as the grandchildren. This isn't daily, it is weekly. But the structure, approach and consistency which flows down to the youngest member is very powerful in keeping family members engaged, supported, and able to achieve their maximum potential.

See for yourself

Do you have a job (even if only part-time)? Can you spot how your leaders work? What would their Leader Standard Work be? Maybe you can even ask them?

- Can you practice LSW yourself? Perhaps with your little brother? Perhaps you are a team leader? Perhaps even at your sports club? Perhaps you are already doing some LSW without knowing about it! Could you do this better.

Psychology and Bias

Psychology is the study of the human mind, it's characteristics, functions and resulting behaviours. How we use our minds has a dramatic effect on how we go about effective problem solving.

Bias can be generally defined as an inclination or prejudice either for, or against, someone or something. Your thoughts and actions are being drawn in one particular direction, other than equally valid, alternate directions.

Psychology

The psychology of problem solving is complex and much remains to be learned. However, as a basic road map, Sternberg proposes that there are meta-components to human intelligence and problem solving. All 'problem solvers' need to go through the following stages:

1. Recognise the existence of a problem
2. Mentally define the nature of the problem,
3. Allocate mental and physical resources to solving the problem
4. Decide how to represent information about the problem
5. Generate problem solving steps
6. Turning the steps in to a workable strategy
7. Monitoring the problem-solving process
8. Evaluating the solution to the problem after a solution is generated

All of these involve our own psychology and have the potential for bias.

Bias

To help us be more self-aware and maximise our problem-solving potential, here are a few pointers:

- For Problem Solving there are four stages:
  1. **Preparation and information gathering**.
  2. **Incubation** (time away from the problem).
  3. **Illumination and insight** (Aha!).
  4. **Verification**. Experience in each stage is important.
- Self-motivation to solve a problem is important. External motivation and reward can create bias.

- In quantitative problems, attribution-judgement training helps. Most people are notoriously poor at judging risk, but risk training with feedback improves results.
- Practice on similar types of problems helps.
- Your mood can make a difference. A sad mood apparently favours detail, whereas a happy mood favours wider creativity. Be aware of this in others too.
- Fixation is a barrier, so deliberate exposure to wider viewpoints helps.
- Incubation time (Delay? Doing something different? Even relaxing in a bath!) can help with seeing new paths to a solution.
- An incremental step-by-step process helps with non-routine problems.
- Walking whilst problem solving or brainstorming in groups up to 4 has been shown to be effective by a Stanford study.
- The use of Toys. The famous creative company IDEO has lots of Toys and gadgets lying around to stimulate thinking.

As Margaret Heffernan says, *"Because we are all biased, and biases are quick and effortless, exhaustion tends to make us prefer the information we know and are comfortable with. We're too tired to do the heavier lifting of examining new or contradictory information, so we fall back on our biases, the opinions and people we already trust."*

You see this sort of bias driven behaviour in organisations regularly. (And you may recognise it in yourself!) Accountants appoint other accountants to senior positions. An employee with a Six Sigma qualification may focus all attention on variation reduction, rather than redesign. A Theory of Constraints mindset will look for the bottleneck, rather than the pacemaker. *"If the only tool you have is a hammer, you tend to see every problem as a nail."* according to Maslow.

Again, this is all evidence of Kahneman's System 1 (fast and automatic) and System 2 (slow, considered and deliberate) thinking.

What we feel is not always real

They say 'the first step is admitting the existence of the problem'. This is easier said than done, especially when we consider something as powerful as cognitive dissonance. How often have we ourselves 'self-justified' a particular behaviour or 're-interpreted information' just to ease that uncomfortable feeling we have about something we've either done, or not done.

How often have you 'been proven right' when being told something we were subconsciously hoping to hear? Yes, you were looking and listening, but were you looking and listening for something in particular? Don't be surprised if you find it quite easily. But what did you miss instead?

How often have you 'fell for it' when being told something by someone you like or respected, or affected by a particular environment or a brand?

Perhaps worse, how often have you missed something, almost blind and deaf to the facts, due to an innate dislike for a particular person or place?

Facts don't care about your feelings. Unfortunately for us, our feelings care about facts. As a result, they can subconsciously affect how we recognise, acknowledge, and sometimes without realising, ignore them.

See for yourself

A good way to be more aware of your own bias is to ask for feedback. Who can you ask for feedback? Ask people who do not look like you, or who are of a different age/gender/race/sexual or political preference. What does this feedback tell you?

Further readings:

Daniel Kahneman, *Thinking, Fast and Slow*, Allen Lane, 2011

Daniel Kahneman, Oliver Sibony and Cass Sunstein, *Noise*, Collins, 2021

Problem Types

Problem Types categorises problems based on how they originally became apparent. It helps us understand how best to respond, and what type of problem-solving approach to take.

In Lean, the problem focus is on improvement, but sometimes when a problem has occurred, it also needs recovery and restoring to its previous state. Sometimes you can anticipate a problem, so prevention is called for.

Below, are the six problem types. Each has typical sources, appropriate responses, and supporting approaches as shown in the table. Types 2, 3, 4, and 5 all should use the scientific method (PDSA).

Type	Sources	Responses	Approaches	Chapters
1	Breakdown	Fix now	Kaizen	
2	Deterioration	Refurbish	TPM, 5S, Kaizen, Standards, Visual, TWI, LSW	Preparing
3	Defect detection and prevention	Stop, prevent	Andon, Poka yoke, A3, Visual, 5 Why, SPC, Six Sigma, Water and rocks,	Working

4	Waste recognition	PDSA, LSW	Kaizen, A3, Kata, Ideas & suggestions, Standards, TWI, Visual, 5 why, Gemba walk, LSW, Water and rocks	Improving
5	Measures, Change initiatives	Value Stream Mapping	Kaizen, A3, VS Mapping, Kata, Hoshin, Supplier partnership, Systems thinking	Improving, Planning and Organising
6	Threat, Opportunity		Design, 3P, Systems thinking, Scheduling, Supplier partnership, Layout and location	Preparing, Planning and Organising

Of course, people are the essential element to effectively solving any of the Problem Types above. Involving the relevant people in discovering the source, agreeing a response, and applying the supporting approach will be key to recovery and improvement. The Chapter on Motivating and Measuring is highly relevant to all the types.

Something else to consider is that most problem solving and innovation relies on building on the work of previous innovations. The popular science writer, Steven Johnson, refers to this as 'the adjacent possible' where ideas and concepts from other fields and areas are adapted to form new innovations. An example is the iPhone that used prior developments in internet, microprocessors, glass, music, data storage, and others to create a revolutionary product. When solving problems, invite outsiders to come see and solicit their views. One of the authors has experienced being pumped for ideas following visits to, for example, Dell and McLaren Formula 1.

Great innovations, the 'change-the-world' type breakthroughs, are very rare. Here scientific thinking (PDSA) is not found. Examples are Newton on gravitation and his laws on force, James Clerk maxwell's 4 equations on electro-magnetism and Charles Darwin on natural selection and evolution.

Problem Types and the use of Critical Thinking

Alvesson and Spicer in *'The Stupidity Paradox'* criticise some for the idea that by being optimistic you can succeed in every aspect of your life. What is needed, they and others maintain, is better critical thinking, or 'negative capability', 'the ability to face up to uncertainty, paradoxes and ambiguities.' To help with this, they suggest:

- **Observe.** Look and listen, including beneath the surface, and avoiding premature problem definition. 'What is going here?'
- **Interpret.** Find out what others think – the perspectives of others – other disciplines, other levels, other players. 'What do the original inhabitants think is happening here?'
- **Question.** 'What are the assumptions we are making, and the reasons behind the assumptions?' 'Why are you interested in this?'

Alvesson and Spicer suggest that 9 processes would be useful to engage in critical thinking:

1. **Reflective routines.** Instead of having ad-hoc Hansei-type sessions, set aside specific regular Reflective sessions. For instance, around 'What have we done this month?'. Also, as per Google, invite outside speakers with provocative viewpoints.
2. **Devil's advocates.** Give specific devil's advocate responsibility to some managers. A specific role to challenge groupthink and the conventional wisdom. This is suggested

by DeBono as one of his '6 Thinking Hats'. (A devil's advocate was used by JFK during the Cuban Missile Crisis.)

3. **Post-mortems.** Build these in, for all cases not just for failures. Make this a routine. Don't miss the opportunity to look back, critically – not just the lip service of 'lessons will be learned'. Avoid personal blame – instead look at the system.

4. **Pre-mortems.** As suggested by Gary Klein. This is essentially a brainstorming session pretending, in advance of starting, that the project has already been implemented and has failed. The idea is to make it safe for dissenters who are knowledgeable about the undertaking and worried about its weaknesses to speak up. It is a proactive approach – taking preventive action.

5. **Newcomers.** Newcomers frequently bring new, fresh ideas. Encourage these to be aired, not suppressed. And the next point...

6. **Outsiders.** As stated by Steven Johnson, most innovations stem from 'the adjacent possible' where breakthroughs result from combining with outside concepts.

7. **Engage your Critics.** Types of bias, wilful blindness and the fundamental attribution error are mentioned in this Chapter. A way to counter this is to give some credibility to your critics.

8. **Competitions and games.** Alvesson and Spicer suggest 'bullshit bingo' where a prize is given for the biggest meaningless statement, to counter gobbledegook speak so common in management, including Lean!

9. **Anti-stupidity task force.** Such a group is tasked with identifying organisational bullshit.

If it isn't broken, don't try to fix it?

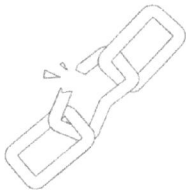

We all experience problems every day. Most are small, like having to change a battery, some require immediate attention, like fixing a leaking tap. Some are quite large, occurring less frequently, like a train driver strike disrupting your travel plans and requiring a change in routine. Some problems occur much less frequently but with significant consequences, like a broken relationship. That's life.

At work and at home, most of us experience a range of problems from small to large. Some problem solutions are aimed at restoration (a repair) others are aimed at improvement (something new, like a new computer.) Sometimes, some problems require creative, out-the-box, thinking.

Some problems are easy to ignore, not to mention to try to categorise. But understanding what type of problem we have can help us massively on our quest to solve it. Thinking critically about current and even potential problems allows us to stay ahead of serious consequences before they present themselves. After all, they say, prevention is better than cure.

Some problems should be solved. Some problems should be left alone. Some problems should not exist at all. Trouble is, we spend most of our time creating and solving problems … in the quest for being busy.

What we focus our energy on finding, is often what gets fixed.

See for yourself

Are you aware how you deal with problems? Do you deal with it right away or do you like to ignore them as much as you can?

- Look at the different problem types. Which one do you recognise the most. What is your 'favourite' problem.

Further readings:

Mats Alversson and André Spicer, *The Stupidity Paradox*, Profile, 2016

Stella Cottrell, *Critical Thinking Skills: Effective Analysis, Argument and Reflection,* Macmillan, 2017

Margaret Heffernan, *Wilful Blindness*, Simon and Schuster, 2011

Stefan Maidan, *The Systems Thinker: A Practical guide to use Critical Thinking for Changing your Life*, Independent, 2020

5 Whys and Root cause

5 Whys is a well-established approach to root cause analysis. It involves the user to simply ask 'why?' successively to answers given, in the quest for establishing the root cause of a problem.

This simple but effective technique really just amounts to a questioning attitude. Never accepting the first answer, always probing behind the answer.

Let's assume a problem has become apparent. Ask why several times, perhaps 3 to 6 times successively. Poor customer service? Why? Deliveries are often late. Why late? Inventory is often out of stock. Why out of stock? Often other products must be made first. There is a queue. Why a queue? Because batches are large, and it takes time to process them. Why large? Because changeover time is long. Why is it long? Don't know. It has never been studied. Voila!

Great if this works. Certainly, try it. Certainly, don't accept the first reason without further probing.

Unfortunately, in practice there is not often one answer to each why. But you should aim at homing in on the crucial 'main cause' by a succession of Pareto analyses. That is, at each stage, focus on the most likely or 'top' reason.

Due to the questioning nature of 5 Why's and the involvement of people, when facilitating this session, it is good to follow a few rules for a more effective use of 5 Why to prevent the session turning into a blame game:

- 'People' reasons for the problem are not acceptable. Remember Deming's 94/6 rule. Most problems lie with the system or the process, not the people. It is just too easy to blame 'people'. What is causing 'the people' to behave in that way?
- Do not allow Whys to become personal or accusing.
- At each Why stage, prioritise. A rule of thumb: don't allow more than two reasons for every why.
- Home in, not home out. For example: We have unreliable machines. Why so? Allow 'Because we don't have regular maintenance'. Do not allow 'Because we have no TPM'. Then further 'Why no regular maintenance?' Allow 'Because maintenance priorities are not clear' but do not allow 'Because no one has worked out a schedule'. In each case, the first answer allows one to be more specific, the second answer runs a risk of widening out the reasons.
- Stop when you get to a reason that is beyond your control of frame of reference. Perhaps there are no ultimate root causes. It just goes on and on. A delivery failure is due to a van running out of petrol, caused by a leaking tank, caused by a weld failure, caused by quality of weld, caused by poor material, caused by cost cutting, caused by financial pressures, caused by...

These cautions, if not taken up, will result in the vague, ultimately unhelpful conclusions such as 'the problem is our people', 'management doesn't get it', 'training is required', or 'we can't fix it because it is outside our scope'.

All this leads onto a structured methodology incorporating the 5 Whys and seeking out the main problem before attempting to implement a solution. Again, here is more from Einstein: *"If I were given one hour to save the planet, I would spend 59 minutes defining the problem and one minute resolving it."*

Why? Because a problem well defined is a problem half solved.

But... Why?

Anyone who either has small children, younger siblings or relatives, or happens to spend a lot of time with them will testify... they ask a lot of questions.

In fact, one of the most famous questions small children tend to ask is "why?".

There is an almost relentless curiosity from small children as to why the situation they are discussing, is as it is. Whilst this is quite charming and fun at the beginning, you soon start to become aware of the 'relentless' side of their quest for truth. They want an answer!

Quite often this endless successive "why?" leads to a final answer from a busy parent or adult "because I said so!" or "because it just is".

But it is indeed this relentlessness that forces us to at least try to answer, and as a result, think in a different way we perhaps hadn't thought of before. We may have lived quite happily with our first couple of answers being the reason behind whatever is being questioned. Perhaps one of the questions leads to you admitting "actually, I don't know why? That's a good point."

When pushed, with the innocent curiosity and determination of a small child, that 'never accepts the first answer', we are forced to 'probe behind the answer to expose underlying causes'. We are forced to go down a path of questioning and thinking we hadn't done before.

It is a very useful attitude to discovering the world and why it is the way it is. It is interesting to wonder at what point we stopped asking so many questions ourselves?

What is your reaction to Einstein's famous quote?

See for yourself

Ask yourself why things are as they are. Can you try this '5 times why' this week in different occasions? Do you get surprising answers?

A3

A3 provides a structure by which a company identifies, frames, acts and reviews progress on problems, projects and proposals.

As a tool, A3 Problem Solving and Reporting, made popular by Toyota, is a way to concisely guide users through the critical problem-solving steps. This involves understanding and clarifying a problem and its root causes, and then identifying countermeasures and experiments to close the gap between the target and the current situation. Note the word 'countermeasure' – a problem is seldom entirely 'solved'.

John Shook describes A3 in his book Managing to Learn as not just a problem-solving process, but a critical part of a management system. The book is an extended case study of interchanges between mentor and mentee that result in homing in on the core problem that was not apparent in the earliest stage. The mentee is continually challenged, not aggressively but with respect, to review his assumptions and data.

John Shook writes:

(A3 is) *"...a visual manifestation of a problem-solving thought process involving continual dialogue between the owner of an issue and others in an organization. It is a foundational management process that enables and encourages learning through the scientific method."*

and:

"It takes two to A3. A3 should not be done alone but as a conversation between manager and subordinate (but better to think in terms of mentor and mentee). The interchanges foster and build wider perspectives and critical thinking. Going through an A3 can be gut-wrenching the first few times and a continuing check on thinking that is too narrow."

Common questions that will be asked in the dialogue include:

- Have you been to the Gemba to see it first hand?
- What do you see as the gap that should be addressed?
- How do you know that?
- That data seems important. Did you check it?
- Would that data be better shown on a graph?
- How did this problem arose?
- Did you ask the customer?
- How will you know if your proposed solution works?
- What do the associates say?

The mentee learns that making mistakes is part of the development process and will not be seen as a reflection on skill or status. We can all learn.

The mentee will often proceed from a jump-in-to-the-obvious problem, to a more considered, fact-based solution. The mentee's scope will often be widened as the problem is viewed from different perspectives. The mentee may develop more of an in-depth appreciation of classic Lean tools, and ways of analysing and presenting data.

An appreciation of 'real' PDCA will be developed. Of course, the mentor must have knowledge and experience of Lean, as well as patience, and a way with words that supports rather than give offence. What a challenge!

Three essential points on A3:

1. A3 is often thought of, or presented, as a problem-solving tool. But, reading the above it will be realised that the A3 steps should be carried out in parallel with

developing the person who is trying to tackle the problem. Learning the associated tools is one thing, but developing a critical, scientific way of thinking is quite another. Too often training and literature on A3 (and Six Sigma DMAIC, and Ford 8D) merely treat these as mechanical or statistical problem-solving steps but say nothing about developing people's ways of thinking along with addressing the problem – including an attitude of reflection, or Hansei.

2. Numerous experiences with the problem solving A3 reveal that most users (at all levels, junior to top) jump to a conclusion as to what the real problem is, and hence the solution. Or they think they know what the problem is and go through the motions of the left-hand side of the A3 to confirm their belief. As you will recognise, this is confirmation bias!

3. In fact, most real-world problems have several possible 'solutions', some of them wide ranging such as 'training', or 'education'. A 'conclusion' like this is too wide and almost useless. But a major aim of the left-hand-side of the A3 is to home in on the 'big-one', to select the most beneficial aspect to tackle first. This means keeping an open mind, and not pre-deciding the aspect to tackle.

An A3 example is shown below for a simple problem of cold coffee at a coffee shop. You will notice that this A3 structure involves Toyota's classic 8 step problem solving methodology. The 8 steps are closely aligned to PDSA (Plan, Do, Study, Act) and to Six Sigma's DMAIC (Define, Measure, Analyse, Improve, Control).

The A3 structure's 8 steps are set out in the table below.

PDSA	Step	Contains	DMAIC
P	1	Clarify the problem	D
		Background	
		Visualise / Gemba	
		Identify the gap	
		Contain	
	2	Break down the problem	M
		5W and 1 H	
		Process chart	
	3	Target setting (SMART)	
	4	Root cause	A
		5 Why	
		4 M's	
D	5	Countermeasures	I
	6	Execution plan	
S	7	Monitor results	
A	8	Standardise and Share	C

A main aim of the left-hand side of an A3 is to home-in on the specific problem. This is highly desirable and guards against widening-out the problem so that, almost inevitably, the result is that the problem becomes unmanageable with conclusions such as 'it's a training problem', 'it's a strategy issue', or 'the problem is lack of direction'. The mentor is supposed to keep the mentee focused and prevent widening out. But beware! A mentor can inadvertently direct the focus towards a particular pre-meditated conclusion. It may be that the mentee, or the A3 problem-solving team, may have an insight into a wider issue that the mentor is unaware of. A problem-solving mentor should always be generous enough to allow the possibility of an unforeseen 'Gee-whiz' or 'Ah-ha' moment for the mentor.

An important point is not the actual 8 step methodology itself, but how the steps are used. If the 8 steps are used in a mechanical way they will be of limited benefit. But if they are seen as vehicles to learn, through coaching and mentoring, this enables another dimension to be realised. Culture change becomes possible. Feedback should be given by the mentor, preferably as soon as possible. This means that there will probably be several sessions of feedback before Step 3 is finalised.

What's the problem?

Solving the wrong problem. We are al prone to this! A service example is working to improve customer response time by cutting a minute or two from an office clerical process, when the real problem is the huge delay caused by a decision to only work once a day on the particular customer problem type. Going to the Gemba to follow through the end-to-end process would reveal this issue.

See for yourself

Can you make an A3 yourself? Choose a subject like a challenge you face in your sportsclub like how do we get more people at the training of how do we win the next championship?

- Or maybe you face a challenge at home? You find you can use a A3 more than you know.

Further readings:

John Shook, *Managing to Learn*, Lean Enterprise Institute, 2008

Durward Sobek and Art Smalley, *Understanding A3 Thinking*, CRC Press, 2012

Theory of Constraints

The **Theory of Constraints** (ToC) by Goldratt is a 5-step problem Improvement Cycle that seeks to identify the single constraint, or bottleneck, in a system with the aim of achieving continuous balanced flow, through that system.

The TOC 5 step problem Improvement Cycle is as follows: Lean practitioners should follow each step in order. Consider, this is a cycle that should be repeated as constraints can and will move as changes to the system are made:

1. **Identify the constraint.** One part of the system is starving, and another part of the system is completely full. This can show itself in lack of inventory or work to process. Or long queues of inventory and too much work to do. Little to no work for periods of time will suggest the constraint is upstream, and too much work in one area would suggest the constraint is either at this point, or downstream from this point.

2. **Decide how to 'exploit' the constraint.** A constraint is precious, so don't waste it. If it is a physical bottleneck, make sure you keep it going, protect it with a time buffer, seek alternative routings, don't process defectives on it, make it quality capable, ensure it has good maintenance attention, ensure that only work for which there is a confirmed market in the near future are processed on it. Here the batch size should be maximised consistent with demand requirements. Use supermarkets that facilitate flow into the constraint.

3. **'Subordinate' all other resources to the constraint.** Encourage flow to the constraint to be as regular and

uninterrupted as possible. This will allow the buffer protecting the constraint (Drum) to be reduced, thereby reducing lead time. Reduce variation in resources immediately upstream of the constraint. Make everyone aware of the constraint's importance. For instance, move inventory as fast as possible after being processed on the constraint, reduce changeover time on non-constraints so as to reduce batch size and improve flow to the constraint, make sure that the constraint is not delayed by a non-constraint (a non-constraint can become a constraint if it is mismanaged). The right batch size at a non-constraint is derived from doing the maximum number of changeovers that time will allow – in other words minimize the batch size and maximise flow.

4. **'Elevate' the constraint.** Break it, but only after doing steps 2 and 3. Buy an additional resource or work overtime on the constraint. If it were a true constraint, this would be worthwhile. Beware, however. It is seldom necessary to break a constraint if steps 2 and 3 are taken. Knowing the constraint is often a valuable piece of information around which planning and control can take place. If you break the constraint, it will move – possibly to a hard-to determine location.

5. **Finally, if the constraint has been broken, go to step 1.** Otherwise continue. Be careful that you do not make inertia the new constraint, by doing nothing.

Holiday hold-ups

How often have you arrived at the airport to depart, and there is only one question on your mind, "I wonder how busy it is?". When you arrive at the front door your first concern has then become a little more focused. "I wonder how busy it is at check – in...". Depending upon various factors, it is either not busy, busy, or very very busy. Assuming it is not so busy, you feel a little more relaxed and turn to your friend and say "I don't think this is going to be so bad after all". Your friend replies "Let's not get too excited, we've got to get through security yet, we don't know how busy it will be there". Your friend knows, there is more than one potential bottleneck before they get to board.

Sure enough, there is a long line of people waiting patiently to pass through security and you immediately start to panic about how 'busy' it is. "Good job we arrived early with plenty of time" you say to your friend.

"How busy" is really referring to how much time this is going to take to pass through this particular step in the process. How long will it take to get all of these other people through this particular point of the airport. Well, it depends on how long it takes to check someone in, and to safely check someone for security. These activities take time, and ideally, exactly the same amount of time. Regardless, they slow down the whole airport experience. You'll notice there are staff there to close gaps in the line and remind you to be ready by removing items whilst in the line such as, belts, laptops, and fluids before you are stood at the checkpoint itself. They know, any time lost at the constraint (the actual checkpoint), is time lost for the whole departure process (system). As one person passes through, they want the next person immediately ready, not a second lost!

We get frustrated when people aren't ready for their checks, or don't have their documents at hand. All these delays, inhibit the effective flow through the constraint, which in turn causes imbalance throughout the entire departure process. Quite often your overall airport experience is really dependent upon on how effectively your chosen airport manages their flow of passengers through various bottlenecks and constraints.

Busy, doesn't have to mean 'stressful' if constraints are identified, managed and balanced flow is achieved.

See for yourself

Identifying constraints is something you can practice. How many constraints do you see this week? Can you use the 5 steps on these constraints? Can you solve them?

Further readings:

Lisa Scheinkopf, *Thinking for a Change: Putting the TOC Thinking Processes to Use*, St. Lucie, APICS, Boca Raton, 1999

Eliyahu M. Goldratt, *The Theory of Constraints*, North River Press, New York, 1990

Projects

A **project** is a set of activities that must be completed to deliver a specific goal within a time frame, using a defined group of resources.

Projects vary in size and scale, with some smaller projects combining and overlapping to achieve a much larger objective. Some projects last days, some weeks, some months.

Projects always have a goal or a clear objective, they have a defined scope (what the project is to do, what it is not to do), and they are almost always bound by time and resource limitations. All projects eventually come to an end as there is an always an agreed completion point or status.

Projects are also an integral part of Agile. Many projects fail or don't work out as planned which is why 'projects' are included in this Chapter.

Project success requires both planning and execution. Planning requires robust realistic thinking. Execution requires competent controlled action. Of course, there are professional project managers, like civil engineers and company takeover specialists but most of us do project management using 'back-of-anenvelope' style. We tend to learn the hard way by having to react to poor planning with last minute adjustments and changes.

Effective management of a project cannot afford to operate this way, and through poor planning and execution, a large proportion of projects fail to meet expectations.

To help us, below are a few insights to consider increasing the success rate of projects through better planning and execution:

- **Lost Lessons learned.** Many projects are similar to other earlier projects. Has the learning, and experience gained, been transferred? "Lessons have been learned' is a statement made following many public project failings. But the 'lessons' seem frequently to be ignored.
- **Potential Problem Planning.** A failure or neglect to think about or anticipate possible future problems. One way to tackle this is to use 'pre-mortems' that pretend that a particular problem has already occurred and then looking back on how it arose, and the responses take.
- **The 'Planning Fallacy'**, studied by several psychologists including Daniel Kahneman, is that project planners often underestimate the time to be taken to complete actions. The planners tend to be overconfident.
- **New Technology Confidence.** Related to overconfidence is the tendency, also studied by several psychologists, to be optimistic about early stages where new techniques or technologies are used, but then pessimistic about later stages. Examples include – AI, process automation, supersonic air travel, and major civil engineering projects.
- **Modelling.** Whilst modelling is not always possible, but is recommended. A model may be a small-scale physical model (say of a service facility, factory, or bridge), or increasingly a 'digital twin'. The latter is really a simulator, long used by NASA for space travel but now increasingly found for factories.
- **Reverse Planning.** Many project plans proceed from start to finish, left to right. But project expert, Bent Flyvbjerg,

recommends the reverse. Begin from the end and work back.

- **The Sunk Cost fallacy.** This can be an issue. Project managers are reluctant to abandon a project because of money that has already been spent on the project. This is invalid. The issue should always be what are the future costs and benefits – past costs are sunk.
- **Minimum Viable Product.** Project management with regard to new products should be strongly influenced by 'minimum viable product' (MVP) practice. Failure is not failure if customer feedback lessons concerning viability are learned early, before major expenditure is incurred.
- **The use of Experiments.** 'Experiments' were discussed in the Improving Chapter. Remember the great inventor Thomas Edison who said he had not failed ten thousand times in the invention of a light bulb, but had found ten thousand material that did not work.

See for yourself

We all have projects. Sometimes the project is a large one, like moving, or even building an extension on house. Some are intermediate, like writing a thesis (or a book!) or a part of a software project. Most projects are small, like planning Christmas dinner, although this one could be a medium size project if 20 people are invited. At the start, the first question is of course, what needs to be done by when? Then follows, who is involved? What do I need? This may even involve 'who' do I need?

What project are you working on right now? For example a project you have as a hobby or in your work.

- How do the insights above help you in this project? Can you improve? Consider increasing the success rate of your project through better planning and execution

Surfacing Problems

Surfacing problems means identifying and analysing issues, challenging assumptions to gain clarity. This leads to better decisions and solutions in various contexts.

"I have no problem" IS the problem !

An organisation can take a passive or an active approach to problems. A passive approach just involves 'wait and see'. If nothing happens – fine. 'If it ain't broke, don't fix it'. If a problem occurs, sort it out. An active organisation – better to call it proactive – tries to identify problems before they occur. This can be done by intervention where a person or manager directs an initiative, or by monitoring a process to give an early indication of impending problems. As an example, take the brakes in your car. You can drive happily until the brake pads wear out and you experience failure – hopefully not fatal. You (or your garage) can check the wear and instigate timely replacement, or your car may have an automatic wear monitoring sensor to give an early warning. From this example, it will be appreciated that pro-active surfacing is not an absolute guarantee against failure but is widely considered to be wise.

In the same way, in an organisation, problems can be deliberately pro-actively surfaced by management intervention, or surfacing can occur as a result of something happening to the process. Examples are given in the table. Generally, Intervention surfacing is top-down (at least in hierarchical organisations), carried out as a result of a management initiative, believing that there is an opportunity for improvement. Process surfacing generally is bottom-up and is initiated by process drift or something in the process performance that has not met expectations.

Examples are given in the table. These are lists, not direct comparisons.

Intervention Surfacing	Process Surfacing
Value Stream Mapping	Reliability-centred maintenance
Kaizen Events	Andon / Line Stop
Supply Chain Mapping	Heijunka / Missed schedule
Inventory Withdrawal	Standard work, 5S
Industrial Engineering	Poka yoke and Jidoka
Six Sigma projects	Daily meetings, Q Circles
A3, Kata	Recording failure demand
Operations Research	SPC
Demand / takt time change	Suggestion schemes?

A process surfacing experience: On a group visit to a Toyota plant, a group member from another automotive company asked: 'How many Andon stops are there per day?' The answer "Over 1,000!". The response 'You obviously have many problems at Toyota!' The answer "We stop for our problems; others ship their mistakes!"

As a non-manufacturing example of process surfacing, consider the recording of Failure Demand. John Seddon defines Failure Demand as demand arising through 'not doing something or not doing something right first time'. The opposite of failure demand is value demand – first time demands for service. Many organisations are simply not aware of how much failure demand there is. In one telecommunications company failure demand was reaching towards 80% of calls. But, of course, failure demand consumes resources. Repeat phone calls must be dealt with. So, an initial step is to record the frequencies of various types of failure demand. Just listen to customers. The results will astound all who have merely treated all demands equally. Failure demand is a systemic problem that requires elimination not reduction.

The response times to issues that have been surfaced, varies:

- Process surfacing, of course, arises at the process. A process failure (such as Line-stop) demands an immediate response. Some process surfacing (such as unsatisfactory 5S, or a missed schedule) are early-warning indications of developing problems. Here, proactive action is appropriate, but it may take time to resolve and improve. Most of these are addressed by bottom-up (or shop floor) actions at the Gemba. However, there are certainly situations that arise at process level that can only be addressed by more senior management.

- Intervention surfacing may arise internally or externally – based on internal information or analysis, 'gut feel', external events, or on opportunity that has become apparent. The response might range from a tactical pivot to a strategic breakthrough. Response time would range from short- to medium-term but seldom immediate.

Do I have a problem?

How do you know that there is a problem?

Often, it is obvious – like a strange noise from your car. Not always. Of course, if you don't know that you have a problem you can't begin to solve it or improve the situation.

Quite frequently, we think, it is easier for an outside person, or friend, to recognise that there is a problem. But a problem with the problem is that the friend may be too embarrassed to say something. At work, you may be afraid to draw attention to a problem. This latter is the topic of psychological safety discussed in the Motivating and Measuring Chapter.

The real problem is when you don't know there is a problem. A leak that goes undetected in your house. A change in speed limits that you didn't realise. And worst, a developing medical condition. With all these, 'the sooner the better'.

Some hidden problems can be 'surfaced' by regular checks.

See for yourself

Do you know how you identify a problem? You can reflect on this on your own or ask others for feedback. This feedback can give you new insights.

Finally

Approaches

As a Fresher you will hear of a host of approaches to the management of operations. This is confusing, not only to Freshers, but also to many seasoned managers. The list of some of the 'biggies' includes:

- Lean, Agile, Six Sigma, Design Thinking, Systems Thinking, and Lean Six Sigma (LSS).
- Partial and application specific approaches include Toyota Production System (TPS), Lean Startup, DevOps, World class.
- Others include MRP and DDMRP, Industry 4.0, Factory Physics, Automation, Additive manufacturing, User story mapping, TQM and FMS.

Each of these approaches have their own advocates, who are often dismissive of other advocates. Each usual has a range of methodologies. Each methodology typically has a company that is most associated with that approach. Some companies have tried, with varying degrees of success, to rebrand the content and make it their own. The truth is, with all these approaches, several have lost their way. However, what is also true is that these approaches have a lot in common at their core.

Therefore, the purpose of this book is to go back to core thinking. To try to remind people that an approach should be simple, engaging and accessible. That some of the way operations education has been delivered in the last 20 years has created obstacles for 'Freshers' by making it more complicated than it needs to be.

Remember that customers don't care what approach you are using – they care about a satisfactory outcome for their requirements.

In this book the focus is on Lean and Agile. This overlapping pair are by far the dominant approaches, and include aspects used in all, or almost all, the wider list of approaches given in the list above. In this book we have taken a deliberatively wide view of both Lean and Agile.

As a Fresher you have great opportunity:

- Simplicity is a common theme in Lean and Agile. Don't be misled by consultants and managers advocating complex solutions. That is why a Fresher's viewpoint is so valuable.
- Several people that you will meet will have outdated ideas. They can be problematical. Please don't be discouraged. 'Hang in there'. You can be the one that eventually helps them 'learn to see'.
- There is a new world (AI, environmentalism, 'Working from Home', demands for work-life balance, reduced prejudices towards men and women), and a shift in the purpose of a commercial organisation – from shareholder maximisation to wider stakeholder benefits. These are groundbreaking opportunities for a Fresher.

Lean and Agile Failures?

Lean and Agile have proved massively effective in many organisations, public and private, that have taken the concepts to heart. However, far too many times, this is not always the case. Lean implementation failure rates have been quoted at anything from 50% to 80%. There are many reasons for this, and some of these we can't help with. In fact, a full list would probably need several pages. However, we have summarised some of the main reasons for failure below.

Each failure type is associated with a typical 'gap' in understanding or behaviour:

- **Organisational politics - a gap in alignment.** Organisational politics is complex and varied which is often beyond our pay grade!
- **Lack of patience - a gap in endurance.** Like Rome, Lean and Agile is not built in a day.

- **Unsuitable strategy and marketing - a gap in internal or external assessment and communication.** Setting out along an inappropriate path is the reason behind many failed businesses.
- **A change in the economy - a gap in the ability to adjust.** The ability to respond to external events can only go so far.
- **Unsuitable products and services - a gap in understanding customer expectations.** Customers ultimately pay the bill and will not continue to do so if unsatisfied.
- **Poor processes - a gap in performance.** A good product using a poor process will fail.
- **Lack of commitment - a gap in sufficient 'drive'.** How do we get everyone motivated?
- **Culture and workforce engagement - a gap in belief and behaviours.** Is the workforce behind what we are trying to do?

Does this mean you shouldn't start working with Lean or Agile? No, of course not, that's not what we're saying. Our experience is that the last five of these failure modes often, at least partially, relate to a misunderstanding of Lean and Agile concepts. This is where we can offer some help.

The Next Horizon

You've finally reached the end of this particular part of your journey. You've been introduced to key concepts and ideas and will hopefully now be able to recognise them all around you. If we've achieved what we aimed for, this was easier than you initially thought, you are engaged, and are possibly wondering how to continue your discovery of Lean and Agile thinking.

It is logical than you will care more about some ideas than others. Some practitioners focus more in one area than others and become specialists. Some prefer a more general approach. Perhaps there are current projects or challenges that require you to 'pull' some of the learning forward and prioritise it that way?

Whichever approach you are more in tune with, don't be afraid to start in one particular area and feed your interest. The priority is that whatever is next, is enjoyable and fun. Lean has so many directions to go in, and now, the possibilities are endless.

Our advice is to reflect on what parts or topics of the book impacted or interested you the most. This is always a good starting point for any next steps. Build on something you have a natural curiosity or even passion for, pull on the thread of discovery. Explore the further reading, then again, search for evidence and examples all around you. Aim to not only understand the concepts, but practice them and involve other people too.

Sharing your learning and understanding, not just in your words but also your thoughts and your actions is a great way to build and finetune your Lean mindset.

Afterall, the next steps present us with great opportunities to further embed the idea that Lean isn't something we can all do – Lean is something we can all be.

So, as Winston Churchill said after the first major victory over the Nazis at El Alemein," This is not the end. It is not even the beginning of the end. But it is perhaps the end of the beginning."

Best wishes on your ongoing journey.

Index

www.ingramcontent.com/pod-product-compliance
Ingram Content Group UK Ltd.
Pitfield, Milton Keynes, MK11 3LW, UK
UKHW020450140825
461782UK00003B/24

9 789082 900811